THE HUMAN RIGHT TO HEALTH

AMNESTY INTERNATIONAL
GLOBAL ETHICS SERIES

General Editor: Kwame Anthony Appiah

In December 1948, the UN General Assembly adopted the United Nations Declaration of Human Rights and thereby created the fundamental framework within which the human rights movement operates. That declaration—and the various human rights treaties, declarations, and conventions that have followed—are given life by those citizens of all nations who struggle to make reality match those noble ideals.

The work of defending our human rights is carried on not only by formal national and international courts and commissions but also by the vibrant transnational community of human rights organizations, among which Amnesty International has a leading place. Fifty years on, Amnesty has more than two million members, supporters, and subscribers in 150 countries, committed to campaigning for the betterment of peoples across the globe.

Effective advocacy requires us to use our minds as well as our hearts; and both our minds and our hearts require a global discussion. We need thoughtful, cosmopolitan conversation about the many challenges facing our species, from climate control to corporate social responsibility. It is that conversation that the Amnesty International Global Ethics Series aims to advance. Written by distinguished scholars and writers, these short books distill some of the most vexing issues of our time down to their clearest and most compelling essences. Our hope is that this series will broaden the set of issues taken up by the human rights community while offering readers fresh new ways of thinking and problem-solving, leading ultimately to creative new forms of advocacy.

FORTHCOMING AUTHORS:

John Broome

Philip Pettit

John Ruggie

Sheila Jasanoff

Martha Minow

THE HUMAN RIGHT
TO HEALTH

Jonathan Wolff

W. W. NORTON & COMPANY

NEW YORK • LONDON

For information about permission to reproduce selections from this book,
write to Permissions, W. W. Norton & Company, Inc.,
500 Fifth Avenue, New York, NY 10110

For information about special discounts for bulk purchases, please contact
W. W. Norton Special Sales at specialsales@wwnorton.com or 800-233-4830

Manufacturing by Courier Westford
Production manager: Julia Druskin

Library of Congress Cataloging-in-Publication Data

Wolff, Jonathan.
The human right to health / Jonathan Wolff. — 1st ed.
p. cm. — (Amnesty International global ethics series)
Includes bibliographical references and index.
ISBN 978-0-393-06335-6 (hardcover)
1. Human rights—Health aspects. 2. World health.
3. Poor—Health and hygiene. I. Title.
RA427.9.W65 2012
362.1—dc23
                                    2011044214

W. W. Norton & Company, Inc.
500 Fifth Avenue, New York, N.Y. 10110
www.wwnorton.com

W. W. Norton & Company Ltd.
Castle House, 75/76 Wells Street, London W1T 3QT

1 2 3 4 5 6 7 8 9 0

To my brothers: Rick, Dave, and Ben.

CONTENTS

THE HUMAN RIGHT TO HEALTH

Introduction

THE HUMAN RIGHT
TO HEALTH DILEMMA

B ooks on global health often start with a nasty shock: a
disturbing detailed example, or bare statistics presented
with a pretense of scientific objectivity. Take the following, unearthed by the Nobel Prize-winning development economist and political philosopher Amartya Sen, in a foreword to
the wonderful book *Pathologies of Power* by medical doctor and
anthropologist Paul Farmer, about whom we will be hearing
more later. In 1990 the median age at death in sub-Saharan
Africa was just five years, which is to say that the number of
infants and young children who died before reaching the age
of five was the same as the number of deaths of everyone who
survived beyond five years.[1] Looking at his source, the World
Development Report for 1993, we see something even more trou-
bling. In Mozambique, Sierra Leone, Guinea, and Afghanistan

the median age of death was a mere two years. This compares to thirty-seven in India, sixty-four in China, and seventy-five in what the report calls "the Established Market Economies."[2]

Very high levels of infant mortality were once a fact of life (if that is the way to put it) everywhere in the world, but they have not been seen for generations in those established market economies. Decent food and housing, as well as modern hygiene and sanitation remove many of the threats to infant health. The assistance of skilled midwives and doctors in birth shrink newborn mortality. And a range of medical techniques, from advanced surgery to simple powders to overcome diarrheal dehydration, can make a huge difference to survival in childhood. We do not need to make new medical discoveries or invent new vaccines or pharmaceuticals to prevent the great majority of the world's infant deaths—or adult deaths, for that matter. So it may seem as obvious as anything that the world community has the moral duty to take action. But what sort of duty is this? And conversely, what sorts of moral claims does each individual have to a full life in good health?

Many theorists and activists now argue that there is a human right to health, and that the early death and recurrent illness of so many millions of people show that this right is being violated on a vast scale. But of course, the claim that there is a human right to health raises a whole host of further questions. Is there really a right to health? What does this actually mean? What does it call for in practice? Even those with good answers to the theoretical questions may feel daunted by the practical issues. Providing essential medical care and keeping people free from disease by providing nutrition, clean water, sanitation, and decent working and housing conditions may not seem much to ask, until we start to think about the cost and who should pay it. General programs to protect people from environmental threats to health and for universal advanced medical care are simply beyond the resources of many, perhaps most, of the countries of the world. Claiming that there is a universal human right to health can seem naive. It is, according to some commentators, utterly unrealistic, even close to dishonest. It has also been argued to be disastrous, diverting countries from systematic, cost-effective, investment in health systems, devoting funds to those who shout the loudest. But the main difficulty is this: how can there be a human right to health if the resources are just not there to satisfy it?[3]

That dilemma is the subject of this book. On the one hand, the reasons for asserting a human right to health seem overwhelming. On the other, a universal human right to health seems impossible to satisfy in the current conditions of the world. Some theorists consequently reject the idea of a human right to health, arguing that we need to approach global health issues in a more pragmatic fashion. Others, more idealistic, have held fast to the idea of a human right to health, arguing that it is too important and basic to be surrendered. Their task is then to work out how to make the human right to health realistic. This book will be an exercise in cautious idealism.

Chapter 1

THE UNIVERSAL DECLARATION OF HUMAN RIGHTS

BACKGROUND

Being imprisoned for a lengthy period without trial, everyone would agree, is a violation of human rights. But it would be a joke, and not a very funny one, to assert that your rights had been violated by several months of unexpected foul weather.[1] Is suffering from ill health more like wrongful imprisonment, or more like an inhospitable climate? After all, falling ill is generally assumed to be a matter simply of bad luck, unless, as it often is, it is a result of your own lifestyle choices.

But consider Moleen Mudimu, who died of AIDS in Zimbabwe in 2006. For the last year of her life she suffered terribly; her flesh wasted away, and her body was covered with sores and fungal infections. The anti-retroviral drugs that would have restored her to a decent level of fitness and significantly prolonged her life were available in the pharmacy at the end of her road. But she was unemployed and had no money to buy them. In any case, purchasing power had been destroyed by the hyperinflation that has been a feature of President Mugabe's chaotic rule. Zimbabwe's previously well-functioning health system had collapsed, and although free treatment was available to a few, demand greatly outstripped supply. So she died.[2] She died, it seems, because of a set of other people's decisions—decisions about the pricing of drugs, patent laws, economic policy, national priorities, and international sanctions. These had structured her environment in a way that made it impossible for her to survive. Paul Farmer calls this "structural violence."[3] Whatever the cause of her condition, it seems perfectly reasonable to say that Moleen Mudimu's human right to health was violated.

To say this much is to make a moral claim. But it is a claim that is also supported in international law. Article 12 of the International Covenant on Economic, Social, and Cultural Rights (ICESCR) begins:

> The States parties to the present Covenant recognize the right of everyone to the enjoyment of the highest attainable standard of physical and mental health.[4]

This covenant, which came into force in 1976, was a way of giving effect to some of the rights set out in the Universal Declaration of Human Rights (UDHR) of 1948, Article 25(1) of which acknowledges a right to medical care.[5]

The Universal Declaration of Human Rights was born out of the trauma of the Second World War. In April 1945, in the last weeks before the German surrender, representatives of fifty nations—primarily the Allied nations that had declared war on Germany or Japan—met in San Francisco with the aim of setting up a new international organization, the United Nations.[6] Some

3,500 delegates, advisers, and staff spent two months drafting the UN Charter and associated protocols. It is said to have been one of the largest international meetings ever to have taken place. The outcome, the United Nations, was designed as an international forum to deal with disputes among nations, to prevent future wars. Notoriously, the general idea had been tried before after the First World War, with the League of Nations, but its failure to preserve peace gave the parties a greater incentive to get the structures right the second time round. US president Franklin Roosevelt felt this especially keenly, and was determined to ensure that the US would ratify the UN Charter, for its failure to do the same thing for the League of Nations had weakened the League beyond hope.

Roosevelt had earlier, in 1941, famously set out what he believed to be the "four freedoms" all humans beings should enjoy: freedom of speech and expression, freedom of worship, freedom from want, and freedom from fear.[7] By the standards of previous declarations of fundamental rights and freedoms, this is an unusual list. Freedom of expression and worship are familiar, but freedom from want and fear stand out as something new. The width of these four freedoms would prove an important inspiration and reference point in drafting the UDHR.

Roosevelt died in April 1945, but momentum began to form behind a human rights agenda for the new United Nations as a shocked world learned of the atrocities of the Nazi regime. Nevertheless, the Great Powers—the US, the UK, and the Soviet Union—were not at all enthusiastic about the idea of an international human rights agreement. After all, the US practiced racial segregation, the UK had a huge, though crumbling, empire, and the Soviet Union had many restrictions on the freedom of its citizens. However, intensive lobbying by Carlos Rómulo of the Philippines, Herbert Evatt of Australia, and philosophy professor Charles Malik of the Lebanese Republic, together with several Latin American states, led to the concerns of less powerful nations and their peoples coming to the fore. Eventually when on June 26, 1945, the UN Charter was completed, it contained provisions for "human rights and for fundamental freedoms for all without distinction as to race, sex, language or religion"—and, crucially, for the foundation of a Human Rights Commission.

Still, it was a long road from the UN Charter of 1945 to the Universal Declaration of 1948. The journey was led through the judicious and inspirational work of Eleanor Roosevelt. But fascinating though it is, this is not the place to retell that story. The points we need to keep in mind are first, that the Universal Declaration has its origins in the shock of the Second World War and in what apparently civilized peoples were capable of doing to one another and to their own citizens, and second, that far from being, as some critics allege, a statement of the principles already followed by the most powerful nations, pressure for universal human rights came from less developed nations. It is amazing that probably every country in the world was, initially at least, in breach of some of the principles it was prepared to endorse.

After innumerable rounds of drafting and redrafting the United Nations finally voted on the Declaration on December 10, 1948. Of the fifty-eight countries that were entitled to vote forty-eight gave their assent, eight abstained—the six members of the Soviet bloc, as well as Saudi Arabia and South Africa—and two were absent. No country voted against, but even more impressively, when the articles were voted on one by one, twenty-three of the thirty were approved unanimously, without abstention. According to Eleanor Roosevelt, the main reason for the abstention of the Soviet Union was that it could not accept the right of everyone to leave his or her country.[8] But generally, the Declaration was much more a testament to the aspirations of the oppressed than it was a protection of the power of the wealthy.

DECLARATIONS, COVENANTS, AND CONSTITUTIONS

Before looking in more detail at the provisions of the Universal Declaration and subsequent covenants, it is worth adding a little more about the origin of another institution which arose in the immediate aftermath of the Second World War, the World Health Organization (WHO). The first chronicle of the WHO, published in 1947, explains its role as an integrated and expanded successor, under the broad framework of the United Nations, to earlier international health organizations.[9] The then pressing concerns facing the international community were expressed in a message of support sent by President Truman to the first International Health Conference held in New York in 1946:

> Modern transportation has made it impossible for a nation to protect itself against the introduction of disease by quarantine. This makes it necessary to develop strong health services in every country, which must be coordinated through international action.[10]

However, in its constitution—which it describes as the "Magna Carta of Health"[11]—the WHO takes itself as having a much wider objective than preventing the international spread of infectious disease:

> The enjoyment of the highest attainable standard of health is one of the fundamental rights of every human being without

distinction of race, religion, political belief, economic or social condition.[12]

And health itself is defined as "a state of complete physical, mental and social well-being and not merely the absence of disease or infirmity."

The Universal Declaration of Human Rights, itself, though, has a rather more muted, if nevertheless very significant, statement (Article 25(1)) which reads:

> Everyone has the right to a standard of living adequate for the health and well-being of himself and of his family, including food, clothing, housing and medical care and necessary social services, and the right to security in the event of unemployment, sickness, disability, widowhood, old age or other lack of livelihood in circumstances beyond his control.[13]

The Universal Declaration recognizes the right to medical care as a determinant of health and well-being, but falls short of the expansive right to health set out by the WHO: it calls for a standard of living "adequate" for health, rather than the "highest attainable standard of health." It is worth noticing that the Declaration implicitly at least makes the vital distinction between medical care and health. A right to a particular level of health is not the same thing as a right to a particular level of *medical care*. For one thing, there are very many determinants of health, such as nutrition and sanitation. Accordingly, it may be possible to achieve high levels of health with relatively little expenditure on medical care, or alternatively, high levels of medical care may not be very effective in achieving decent population health. As the Declaration implies, a commitment to health, ideally, requires attention to those factors that will keep people well, rather than merely on the factors such as medical care that may help restore them to health when they fall sick.

However, the story does not stop here. The Declaration was just that: a declaration. Separate discussions were needed to create a binding covenant, and it soon became apparent that not all countries would be prepared to commit themselves to legally binding economic and social rights, as contrasted with less controversial political and civil rights. In 1954, drafts of two covenants were finally completed, one on civil and political rights and the second on economic, social, and cultural rights. It was not until 1966, however, that the covenants were adopted by the UN, and they did not come into force as a formal part of international law until as late as 1976, when they had been ratified by the required number of countries. The first, the International Covenant on Civil and Political Rights (ICCPR), though highly significant, proved rather less contentious, in protecting individuals from forms of discrimination, oppression, and persecution. It has been ratified by the great majority of nations of the world.[14] The second, the International Covenant on Economic, Social, and Cultural Rights (ICESCR), has encountered more opposition, and has been ratified by rather fewer countries; indeed, the USA has not done so. But it is this covenant that primarily interests us as it sets out, in Article 12, an elaborate statement of the human right to health:

> 1. The States parties to the present Covenant recognize the right of everyone to the enjoyment of the highest attainable standard of physical and mental health.
> 2. The steps to be taken by the States parties to the present Covenant to achieve the full realization of this right shall include those necessary for:

(a) The provision for the reduction of the stillbirth-rate and of infant mortality and for the healthy development of the child;

(b) The improvement of all aspects of environmental and industrial hygiene;

(c) The prevention, treatment and control of epidemic, endemic, occupational and other diseases;

(d) The creation of conditions which would assure to all medical service and medical attention in the event of sickness.[15]

Two years after the Covenants came into force, in 1978, an International Conference on Primary Health Care took place in Alma-Ata, then in the USSR, now in Kazakhstan. The resulting declaration, signed by 134 countries, began by summarizing the WHO position that:

health, which is a state of complete physical, mental and social well-being, and not merely the absence of disease or infirmity, is a fundamental human right and that the attainment of the highest possible level of health is a most important world-wide social goal whose realization requires the action of many other social and economic sectors in addition to the health sector.[16]

Section 5, however, illustrates the dangers in setting targets, even if they are twenty-two years away:

A main social target of governments, international organizations and the whole world community in the coming decades should be the attainment by all peoples of the world by the year 2000 of a level of health that will permit them to lead a socially and economically productive life.

The Alma-Ata conference gave impetus to the right-to-health movement, which was beginning to find its feet.[17] What, though, should we say about countries that have not ratified the conventions? Consider, for example, a country that has not ratified the Covenant on Civil and Political Rights. Suppose we then find it is torturing members of the political opposition, and that the international community voices strong protest about human rights abuses. It would hardly seem an adequate response if the president of the country were to respond that the opponents are making a simple legal mistake: human rights conventions are not binding on countries that have not ratified them, and so there are no relevant human rights to violate. Rather, we are likely to believe that such rights now form part of what can be called "international customary law": morally and legally binding on all countries once there is significant international weight behind them, whatever an individual state's attitude. In this view, human rights conventions are binding on all nations in the way in which domestic law is binding on all citizens, whether or not they have personally consented to those laws.

PROGRESSIVE REALIZATION AND CORE OBLIGATIONS

The human right to health is now an established part of international law. Yet looking at the terms in which these declarations and conventions are stated, one may be filled with a sense of hopelessness. What could it mean to guarantee to all the people of the world "the right to the highest attainable standard of health," especially according to the WHO definition of "complete physical, mental and social well-being"? Does everyone in the world have the right to the health and life expectancy of the

Japanese, who currently, as a nation, have the longest life expectancy? How could that be achieved? And do even the Japanese enjoy "complete physical, mental, and social well-being," especially in light of natural events beyond human control such as the earthquake and tsunami of March 2011? Without a huge increase in budgets, which is not in prospect, attempting to provide everyone with even a more modestly defined right to health could drain resources from other vital areas, such as education and housing. Many critics will view such conventions as no more than fine words and sentiments.

In recognition of the difficulty of resource constraints, the ICESRC adopts the notion of "progressive realization" rather than "full immediate realization" of the rights.[18] In 2000 this was further clarified when the Committee on Economic, Social, and Cultural Rights issued the very important General Comment 14 to explain how the human right to health can be approached in practice. The committee, which was constituted in 1985 to monitor compliance with the ICESCR and to issue guidance on its interpretation, understood the difficulties of the task, acknowledging, in Article 5, that the full enjoyment of the right to health is a "distant" and in fact "receding" goal for many millions of people.[19]

Accordingly, General Comment 14 states that the right to health is not the right to be healthy (Article 8). Nevertheless, the right to health is not merely the right to medical care, which is merely one of the many determinants of health. Healthy living and working conditions, for example, are just as vital (Article 11).

The most important issue is that of resource constraints, and it is accepted that there can be legitimate reasons why a state may not be able fully to realize the right to health. Hence the committee adopted the language of "progressive realization," which means that a country must take planned and targeted steps toward full realization, but cannot be criticized for not immediately achieving the highest standard of health for its people if that is not attainable. General Comment 14 insists that:

> 30. . . . States parties have immediate obligations in relation to the right to health, such as the guarantee that the right will be exercised without discrimination of any kind (art. 2.2) and the obligation to take steps (art. 2.1) towards the full realization of Article 12 [of the Covenant on Economic, Social and Cultural Rights]. Such steps must be deliberate, concrete and targeted towards the full realization of the right to health.

The earlier General Comment 3 had clarified the notion of a state's "minimum core obligations." In the present context, this instructs that states must use whatever resources they have to supply essential primary health care.[20]

The position, however, remains somewhat confusing. "Progressive realization" permits a country's limited resources to provide a valid excuse for limited progress to full realization, whereas the notion of "minimum core obligations" suggests that there is no excuse for failing to achieve a particular level of health care. It may seem that these ideas flatly contradict each other. A very poor country may not be able to provide even basic primary care for all. Does it thereby breach the human right to health of its citizens? But if it can do no more, what purpose can be served by accusing it of human rights violation (as General Comment 3 tacitly admits)? Or is the point that it must seek international assistance, and in signing up to ICESRC wealthy nations have accepted their responsibilities to assist poorer nations in meeting their minimum core obligations? This, in fact, is what General Comment 14 suggests. But it raises one of the central philosophical and legal questions regarding the doctrine of human rights. It is all very well to argue for universal human rights, but who or what has the responsibility to meet those rights, especially when it can be very expensive to do so? This question will preoccupy us throughout this book.

One further development is of particular interest. In 2005, General Comment 17, on the right to benefit from scientific progress, was issued. The committee accepted that there is a human right to benefit from intellectual production, but at the same time points out that particular regimes of copyright law are constructed for social benefit. A pressing concern regards general access to patented medicines. Do states have an obligation to protect intellectual property even if this means that thousands may die prematurely? This, of course, has become the issue of "access to essential medicines" which will also be a recurring theme in this book.[21]

In summary, the human right to health is now a well-established part of international law, although with some elements in need of further refinement, especially concerning the ideas of progressive realization and core obligations. Having the human right to health inscribed in international law is a vitally important achievement. But it is not enough to silence all critics. What, after all, are the moral foundations of the human right to health? And what does it call for in practice? We will take up these important questions in the next chapter.

Chapter 2

THE HUMAN RIGHT TO
HEALTH AND ITS CRITICS

RIGHTS, HUMANITARIANISM, AND POWER

We saw in the last chapter that the UDHR gave rise to two separate covenants. The first, on civil and political rights, has been very widely ratified, while the second, on economic and social rights, including the right to health, has encountered more resistance, especially from the USA, although most other countries have now ratified it. The rights of the first covenant—rights to freedom of expression, against arbitrary arrest, imprisonment, and torture—are primarily "negative" rights of non-interference. These are often called "first-generation" rights. "Second-generation" social and economic rights require much more than non-interference. They require action, but action by whom? It does not seem plausible to think that every human being has the right to call on every other human to provide everything set out in the ICESCR, such as the right to education, or, indeed, the right to health. Most of these duties will, in the first instance, fall on the state, and ultimately on the burdened taxpayer.

The argument, however, that first-generation rights are cheap and easy to enforce, and second-generation rights prohibitively expensive, has now been thoroughly discredited.[1] The cost of enforcing rights of non-interference can be enormous. For example, each of us has human rights to liberty and security. The state has a duty not to undermine our liberty and security, but also to protect us from violations of these rights by other citizens. Such protection requires criminal and civil justice systems with vast resources devoted to the police, the law courts, and prisons, not to mention the military. It may well be cheap for the state not to interfere, but not at all cheap for it to stop others from doing so, and to provide systems of punishment and compensation. The real reason for a reluctance to endorse second-generation rights is probably an ideological position that it is not for the state to guarantee extensive economic and social rights for its citizens.

In addition, some theorists have worried about "rights inflation." As first-generation rights, such as the right to freedom of speech and against arbitrary arrest, are so very important , it could be a mistake to add other rights, as the more rights there are the more devalued the currency of rights will become. If the notion of a human right is stretched thin, so it is alleged, no human right will be taken seriously.[2] And yet another source of reluctance is vagueness. What do the second-generation rights actually call for in practice? To take the example that is our subject here, what can the right to health—the right to the highest attainable level of health—actually mean?

Given these problems, insisting on a right to health looks like a hard road to travel. Why attempt it? The global burden of disease is immense, but many moral arguments are available to support calls upon governments and international organizations to act. Human beings already have moral duties of charity and of humanitarian assistance. Why, then, complicate matters by talking about rights to health?

But rights can make a difference. The key point is that rights concern the distribution of power and status. Those with rights have enforceable claims, and need not rely simply on the goodwill of others.[3] By contrast, to need humanitarian aid is often taken as a sign of weakness and dependence while to be able to offer it is a sign of strength and superiority. There can be little better illustration of this than the perhaps apocryphal story of Soviet Union schoolchildren in the 1970s being encouraged by the authorities to donate their kopeks to provide charity for the downtrodden poor of the USA, as a way, most likely, of presenting an image of a particular world ranking of states.[4]

The distinction between rights and humanitarian aid is important. Humanitarian aid is, in a sense, conservative: it conserves existing power structures, whereas to recognize another's rights is to cede authority to them, at least within a particular sphere. And who knows, they might use that authority in ways in which you'd rather they didn't, for example as many postcolonial states did when they finally gained independence and had the chance to elect their own governments.[5] For this reason, one can see why powerful states, though they might be perfectly happy to offer humanitarian aid, may wish to stop short of recognizing the rights of countries or peoples that are in a dependent position.

Rights arguments are also more powerful in that while humanitarian arguments typically address only temporary urgent needs, rights arguments can also concern broader structures of liberties and opportunities. Although nothing is infallible, the point of establishing rights is to try to rebalance the power relationship, and to produce long-term, reliable structures that will remove the need for humanitarian concern in the future. That, at least, is the hope, and that is why rights are worth pressing for, even when humanitarian aid is, for the moment, forthcoming.

RIGHTS AND HUMAN RIGHTS

These last comments primarily concerned relations between states. Yet the same points apply to a government's relationship to its citizens. Rights give permanence and power, whereas humanitarianism seems uncertain and temporary. We are all better off and more secure with rights to government action rather than hoping for the government's continued goodwill. But we now need to turn to the more detailed question of the difference between a right and a human right, especially in relation to health.

Many slip between rights talk and human rights talk without marking the difference, as from time to time we will do in this book. Legalistically, of course, human rights could be thought of as simply those rights declared to be human rights in international treaties and declarations. But in the drafting of the Universal Declaration on Human Rights it became clear that something else was at stake. Essentially human rights have a double role. On the one hand, they provide a statement of the minimum moral obligations owed to human beings simply by virtue of their existence as human beings. On the other, they generate a mechanism of accountability beyond the nation-state. If a country violates the human rights of its citizens, then those outside national boundaries should sit up and take notice. To enshrine something as a human right is to open up the internal affairs of a country to international scrutiny. As one of the leading drafters of the UDHR, Charles Malik, of Lebanon, put the point in a speech to the United Nations General Assembly on the day the assembly was to vote on whether to adopt the Declaration: "I can agitate against my government, and if she does not fulfill her pledge, I shall have and feel the moral support of the whole world."[6]

To say that human rights make a country accountable to the international community does not yet say what form that accountability should take. At one end of the scale, it is a matter of "opening the books" through forms of audit, report, or inspection. At the other end, for very serious human rights violations, it may even be that military action will be called for. And in between there are many other mechanisms. "Naming and shaming" is a popular approach in relation to the human right to health, used, for example, by the French organization Médecins Sans Frontières and the US-based Physicians for Human Rights, which has publicized harms to health experienced in, for example, the Chilean dictatorship, Israel's occupation of the West Bank, and the first Gulf War, using such techniques as epidemiological studies and DNA analysis of mass graves.[7] Other possibilities include diplomatic communications, sanctions, and, most importantly, positive assistance.

Contrast the international function of human rights with rights granted by a government on such things as pensionable age. In the UK, as I write, citizens are entitled to a state pension at the age of sixty-five. This is a right. However, the government has recently introduced a change to the law so that in the future pensionable age will rise, and it is likely that further changes will adversely affect current workers. Some people may feel that in changing the law in this way the government is ignoring, perhaps even violating, the rights of its citizens, and trade unions have started to campaign on this basis. But whether the pensionable age in the UK is sixty-five, sixty-six, sixty-seven, or sixty-eight seems to be a matter purely for the UK to decide. It is none of the business of the international community. However, if the UK allowed its elderly citizens to live in squalor, it seems plausible that the international community should be entitled to start asking questions, and, if the answers are unsatisfactory, express its disapproval. Hence, one may say, this is evidence that there is no human right to a pension at any particular age, but that there is a human right to dignified retirement and old age. If a government ignores its obligations, such as by allowing state and private providers of care homes to treat elderly people with contempt, or leave them in degrading conditions, it can justly be subject to international scrutiny and censure.

PHILOSOPHICAL CHALLENGES

As we noted, the covenants are full of fine words. But do they really have substance?[8] Although the language of human rights is relatively new, the idea of a human right is closely related to the older notion of a natural right. John Locke (1632–1704), one of its most powerful philosophical advocates, set out to refute the feudal idea that, in effect, human beings were subjects, not citizens. In the feudal view, any rights enjoyed by individuals are granted by their superiors, who in turn received their title from the king or sovereign. The sovereign, appointed by God, ruled by divine right, and had the right of arbitrary power over all of his subjects. Nothing the sovereign did, in this view, could be understood as a violation of the rights of his or her subjects. Locke aimed to establish the truth of the reverse of this: human beings have natural rights that even the sovereign must respect. Furthermore, sovereign power was granted only through a social contract with the people, and if the sovereign overstepped the limits set out by the natural rights of the people, rebellion could sometimes be justified. Hence, Locke suggested, human beings have natural rights to "life, liberty and estate."[9]

The doctrine of natural rights is one foundation of modern liberal democracy, and is credited with influencing the constitution of the United States, and the ideas that underpinned the French Revolution. Yet the doctrine of natural rights in turn suffered radical criticism. Notoriously, Jeremy Bentham, commenting on the French Declaration of the Rights of the Man and of the Citizen (1789), argued that "natural rights is simple nonsense . . . natural and imprescriptible rights . . . nonsense on stilts."[10] (By "imprescriptible" Bentham probably meant "inalienable," i.e. rights that cannot be waived by their possessor or taken away.) Bentham's argument was that "rights are the child of the law," and so a natural right—a right prior to the law—was a nonsensical idea, strictly speaking self-contradictory.[11]

Arguments like these are uncomfortable and will worm away at us unless we address them properly. What, after all, are the foundations of human rights? What are the arguments for believing in them? In fact, there are many arguments: that they are based on our common humanity, or on human dignity, or on our nature as human agents, or on our basic needs, or even on God's will. Our problem is not that there are no foundations for human rights, but that there are too many. Which is the correct account of the foundations? We are unlikely to be able to find a conclusive, universally convincing, single argument or account.

This, however, repeats a debate that took place in the context of drafting the Universal Declaration. For what is as true now as sixty years ago is that there is much greater agreement on the broad list of human rights than there is on their moral foundations. Of course, there are disagreements about content, but the convergence on doctrine is remarkable, given the divergence on foundations. Jacques Maritain, a French philosopher who played a role in the preparations for the Declaration and observed many drafting meetings, famously commented:

> During one of the meetings of the French National Commission of UNESCO at which the Rights of Man were being discussed, someone was astonished that certain proponents of violently opposed ideologies had agreed on the draft of a list of rights. Yes, they replied, we agree on these rights, *provided we are not asked why* [emphasis in original].[12]

To use terminology from political philosopher John Rawls, the Universal Declaration of Human Rights may be seen as analogous to Rawls's idea of an "overlapping consensus," in which each person can endorse a political doctrine for his or her own moral reasons.[13] In sum, then, there are many moral reasons for human rights. People can agree on the Universal Declaration, but they endorse it for a whole range of moral reasons. This, perhaps, explains the appeal of human rights doctrine within a broadly liberal framework, in that it does not presuppose that everyone accepts the same basic moral theory.

But what do we do about residual differences in interpretation? The "overlapping consensus" is far from perfect. At the level of detail there is no consensus. Probably the right response at this point is simply to acknowledge the limits of philosophical argument, and allow the resulting disputes to be resolved through the development of democratic politics and legal doctrine.[14]

A quite distinct line of opposition to rights-based arguments, associated with Hegel and Marx and with communitarian and feminist thought, suggests that there is something wrong with any culture in which people express their moral relations to one another in terms of rights.[15] For, so the argument runs, a rights-based moral discourse presupposes a society of conflict and disagreement that we would do well to avoid. It is only necessary to claim a right if there is a potential or actual dispute.

While it is hard to deny that having no conflict would be a superior way to live, in practice we are stuck where we are, in a society where, sadly, there is conflict over many things, and especially the use of resources. Hence, like it or not, we need rights to navigate our way through competing claims. Still, the objector has a further point to make. While it is true that we may well need rights, nevertheless, we have a choice as to how much we rely on rights claims in making our arguments. A quick recourse to rights will heighten the sense of conflict and encourage a legalistic culture in which people encounter one another as opponents, rather than as fellow citizens.[16] If I think you have something that belongs to me, I could politely ask for it back, or I could instruct my lawyer to serve a writ on you for its return. A society where people routinely do the latter is highly unappealing. But nevertheless, in the world in which we live, conflict exists and assertion of rights, however regrettable, is sometimes indispensable.

A more common criticism is that human rights are an extension of values appropriate to some regions of the world but not all. In particular, it is sometimes said that the doctrine of human rights is a Western notion and there is something suspect, even imperialistic, in attempting to apply it to the entire world as a whole.

This objection was of pressing concern to the drafters of the

Universal Declaration of Human Rights, and, notoriously, it was expressed in forceful if rather condescending terms by the American Anthropological Association in a submission to the commission:

> How can the proposed Declaration be applicable to all human beings, and not be a statement of rights conceived only in terms of the values prevalent in the countries of Western Europe and America? . . . If we begin, as we must, with the individual, we find that from the moment of his birth not only his behavior, but his very thought, his hopes, aspirations, moral values which direct his action and justify and give meaning to his life in his own eyes and those of his fellows, are shaped by the body of custom of the group of which he becomes a member. The process by means of which this is accomplished is so subtle, and its effects are so far-reaching, that only after considerable training are we conscious of it.[17]

The AAA did not go as far as recommending that the drafters give up their task. Rather, it recommended that the Declaration give great emphasis to cultural difference and the right of people to live in accordance with the moral understandings of their own group. And much later, in 1999, the AAA issued its own declaration, which endorses other human rights declarations and conventions while helpfully noting that "Human rights is not a static concept. Our understanding of human rights is constantly evolving as we come to know more about the human condition."[18] The American Anthropologists, then, have come to accept the UDHR as a basis for their own position, and thus have satisfied themselves that the doctrine of human rights need not be seen in terms of Western imperialism."[19]

Concerns of cultural imperialism will never entirely be put to rest.[20] Although the drafting committee included representatives from many countries of the world, there were no representatives from sub-Saharan Africa, with the exception of (white) South Africa. Furthermore, several of the representatives of non-Western countries were people who had lived or studied in the West and so may be treated with suspicion. This chink of vulnerability has led to a more recent attack on the doctrine of human rights as privileging "Western values" over "Asian values."[21]

The "Asian values" issue came to prominence in 1993 when countries such as Singapore, Malaysia, and Indonesia, who had been Cold War allies of the West, joined with over thirty other Asian states in a conference in Bangkok prior to the landmark World Congress on Human Rights taking place later that year in Vienna. The Bangkok conference gave rise to a declaration which, while reaffirming strong commitment to the UDHR, enters some qualifications. After several clauses of apparent enthusiastic endorsement of the international human rights regime, the following appears:

> *Noting* the progress made in the codification of human rights instruments, and in the establishment of international human rights mechanisms, while *expressing concern* that these mechanisms relate mainly to one category of rights.

This cryptic comment is not explained, but soon after there appears a subtly worded trio of observations:

> *Reaffirming* the principles of respect for national sovereignty, territorial integrity and non-interference in the internal affairs of States,

> *Stressing* the universality, objectivity and non-selectivity of all human rights and the need to avoid the application of dou-

ble standards in the implementation of human rights and its politicization,

Recognizing that the promotion of human rights should be encouraged by cooperation and consensus, and not through confrontation and the imposition of incompatible values . . .[22]

Further on, the document places emphasis on economic development and trenchantly draws attention to the gap between wealthy and poorer nations as an obstacle to the enjoyment of human rights. However, there is little sign of the affirmation of values that are contrary in spirit to those of the human rights movement. Indeed, the declaration goes on to reaffirm the human rights of women and children in terms that are perfectly consistent with many other human rights declarations. Still, there are further elements of the declaration that are in stark contrast to the general understanding of the role of human rights, most notably:

4. *Discourage* any attempt to use human rights as a conditionality for extending development assistance;
5. *Emphasize* the principles of respect for national sovereignty and territorial integrity as well as non-interference in the internal affairs of States, and the non-use of human rights as an instrument of political pressure;

If, as we have suggested, the whole point of a doctrine of human rights is to open up the internal affairs of a country to forms of scrutiny and persuasion by other countries and their citizens, then to take these ideas seriously is really to abandon the doctrine of human rights. The general tenor of the document is to affirm a role for international cooperation in providing economic and technical development assistance, but to ward off international attempts to "police" human rights. It also hints at the hypocrisy of the developed nations. In partial support of this last allegation we should note that it was only as late as 1992, one year before the Bangkok Declaration, that the US had ratified the International Covenant on Civil and Political Rights, and it did so with so many reservations and exceptions that the Covenant is often considered to be effectively unenforceable with respect to the United States.

At the Vienna conference itself, the "Asian values" debate was given sharper focus, with numerous forceful interventions by representatives of East Asian countries. According to one observer, the foreign minister of Singapore warned that "universal recognition of the ideal of human rights can be harmful if universalism is used to deny or mask the reality of diversity."[23] Going much further, the spokesman for China's foreign ministry is said to have asserted that "individuals must put the state's rights before their own."[24]

Here, perhaps, we see an elucidation of the earlier comment from Bangkok, that human rights instruments have concentrated on "one category" of rights: those of individuals, leaving out the rights of states. It seems to be implied that Asian values require much more attention to the rights of states, even at the expense of the rights of individuals.

Amartya Sen provides a fascinating, and very measured, response to this combination of criticisms. He points out that it is, in a way, naive and Eurocentric to generalize about "Asian values." Asia represents 60 percent of the world's population and contains many diverse traditions, religions, and cultures. Furthermore, any individual may well have multiple identities and allegiances.

Sen elegantly argues that in all traditions—East and West—

the elite have always asserted their right to freedom. The modern drive of Western liberalism is to try to spread such freedom throughout society as a whole. Sen finds considerable evidence that the ancient philosophical traditions of China, and even more so India, are complex and contain traditions of freedom and toleration alongside traditions of authoritarianism. In this respect they barely differ from Western traditions.[25]

To return to the Bangkok Declaration, part of its argument is that the needs, rights and liberties of the peoples of the East have been ignored by powerful Western states. This, though, is not an argument against the Western values of human rights. Rather, it is an argument for their application on a non-hypocritical basis; the Bangkok Declaration itself warns of a "double-standard." The letter of the Universal Declaration, as we saw, is one of protection of the weak, not of the privilege of the strong, and the Bangkok Declaration is a reminder of this essential point. The other major issue hinted at by the authors of the Bangkok Declaration, and forcefully reasserted in Vienna, is that the Asian states greatly resent interference by other countries in their own affairs. But then, they are hardly alone on this matter. One would not say that the United States welcomes outside criticism, pressing very hard on the idea of its own sovereignty, and is not at all open to the idea that it should be held accountable for alleged human rights abuses, such as claims that it has used methods of torture. Yet we need to keep reminding ourselves that the whole point of human rights is to provide a counterbalance to state sovereignty, as, tragically, was absent in Europe in the 1930s and early 1940s. This will always be uncomfortable, especially for those in power, but it is precisely why there is no room for a declaration of states' rights in a declaration of human rights.[26] The peoples of Asian states need, and are entitled to, human rights as much as people from the West. Nevertheless, as the American Anthropologists insist, there is considerable room for different countries to implement human rights in ways that are most culturally appropriate.

GENERAL COMMENT 14

Before looking in detail at real-life questions of the human right to health, it will be helpful to look a little more at General Comment 14, which we introduced in the last chapter, to understand in more detail how it attempts to clarify what the human right to health means in practice.

We have already identified some of the key features of General Comment 14, such as the ideas of progressive realization and core obligations, and we have noted that the right to health is not the right to be healthy, for no one could have that right. Contingencies of biology and life mean that we are all vulnerable to illness, whatever resources we have available. At the same time, the right to health is not merely the right to medical care, for this is only one of the many determinants of health. The right to health seems to stand somewhere between the right to medical care and the right to be healthy. What, then, could it be? Philosopher Henry Shue has clarified the idea of a human right as giving protection against a series of what he calls "standard threats."[27] The human right to health, then, gives individuals protections against "standard threats to health": a vague idea, perhaps, but one that at least provides a focus for discussion.

General Comment 14 can be seen as elucidating the standard threats against which everyone should be guaranteed protection. In effect, it sees the right to health as constituted by a series of obligations on governments, and the document helpfully sets out a number of what it calls "interrelated and essential elements" that underpin the right to health. These elements describe the features of a well-functioning health system. First, there is the element of *Availability*. Naturally enough, this suggests that public health and health care facilities must be sufficient in number to meet the needs of the population. It is explicitly stated that such facilities include not only hospitals, clinics, essential medicines, and adequately paid medical staff, but also safe drinking water and adequate sanitation.

Next comes *Accessibility*, which in this case is split into four dimensions: non-discrimination; physical accessibility in the sense of being in safe physical reach (including water and sanitation); economic accessibility, in the sense of affordability, for all including the economically most disadvantaged; and "information accessibility," concerning the provision of health-related information to the general public. The element of accessibility is very wide-ranging. For example, it is sometimes noted that in parts of the developing world many people have to travel some distance to access water and toilet facilities. Often the routes are unsafe, particularly for women and girls, and leave them vulnerable to attack and sexual assault. There are many things that can be said about such a situation, but among its many failings, General Comment 14 makes clear that it is a violation of the government's duty to protect the human right to health.

The third element is *Acceptability*, which requires that medical facilities and services meet standards of medical ethics, and are "culturally appropriate, i.e. respectful of the culture of individuals, minorities, peoples and communities, [and] sensitive to gender and life-cycle requirements": a complex matter. The fourth and final element, naturally enough, is *Quality*; doctors must be well-trained, machinery should function properly, medicines must not be past their use-by date, and so on.

It is one thing to lay out the elements of an ideal system, and another to understand how those elements are to be achieved. General Comment 14 also attempts to specify what governments must do in terms of concrete action. As human rights doctrine evolved, it has become common to divide government obligations into three types: the duty to respect, the duty to protect, and the duty to fulfill. General Comment 14 follows this pattern. The "respect" element concerns a series of direct relations between the government and its citizens. Governments should not discriminate in offering medical and health-related services, by, for example, excluding members of an ethnic minority from health care. Governments should not impede traditional medicine, or allow the marketing of unsafe drugs. They should not force coercive treatments upon people except in some cases of mental illness or communicable disease. They should refrain from limits on contraception and they should not withhold health-related information. They should not pollute the environment or test nuclear weapons if this leads to unsafe release. And they must not limit health service access as a punitive measure.

The longer a list, the more problems there are likely to be. For example, if a government believes that a traditional medicine is unsafe, it appears to have conflicting duties. And though many would agree that restricting access to contraception is to breach human rights, this is hardly universally shared. These examples remind us again that not everything is settled within human rights doctrine. However, although many of these provisions seem bland and unexceptional, it is not until one looks at what might be taken for granted that it is possible to see that many breaches of the human right to health may not even be noticed. For example, is it always the case that prisoners are provided with access to health services on the same terms as other citizens? Although in some countries, paradoxically, it may be easier to obtain medical attention when in prison than outside, still it may be part of the mind-set of prison guards and governors that prisoners should be allowed to suffer greater health problems than others as part of their punishment. But according to General Comment 14, to deny treatment for punitive purposes is to breach human rights. And the requirements of non-discrimination are interesting too. For example, many countries like to concentrate highly equipped hospitals in urban centers, which can mean diverting resources from elsewhere. Does this discriminate against those who live in rural areas? Respecting the right to health is not a straightforward matter.

The second wave of duties comes under the heading of the duty to protect. This places duties on the state to ensure that no other party interferes with the citizen's right to health. Examples include ensuring that private health provision does not undermine equitable access for all, and the licensing and regulation of medical professionals. It also includes protection from "harmful social or traditional practices," and, to quote:

> States are also obliged to ensure that harmful social or traditional practices do not interfere with access to pre- and post-natal care and family-planning; to prevent third parties from coercing women to undergo traditional practices, e.g. female genital mutilation; and to take measures to protect all vulnerable or marginalized groups of society, in particular women, children, adolescents and older persons, in the light of gender-based expressions of violence.

This, of course, is a minefield. Some have argued that what the General Comment calls "female genital mutilation"—which, they say should be described in more neutral terms as "genital cutting"—is a legitimate cultural practice and therefore its prohibition is a violation of other human rights. Similarly, many have argued from a religious perspective that contraception, and even more so, abortion, are morally unacceptable, and so not only is it right to restrict access to services and information about them, but it is even wrong to offer them. Once more, this shows that there are controversies even within human rights doctrine, and it may be wondered if the committee was sensible or entitled to take such a bold line on a controversial question, whether or not one agrees with the line it takes. The United States, for example, has complained that General Comment 14 has expanded the human right to health beyond its initial basis in an arbitrary and unaccountable fashion. According to the US:

> General Comment 14 . . . expresses the opinions of individuals acting in their private capacity, and is not the result of deliberations among States. The United States does not consider these types of documents to have any standing in international fora.[28]

We have seen, then, how General Comment 14 deals with the obligations to respect and protect. Next we must explore the duty to fulfill, which sets out a whole series of positive obligations for states, beyond anti-discrimination (respect) and safeguarding against the interference of third parties (protect). The basic idea of the duty to fulfill is, of course, to give effect to the right to health in national, political, and legal systems. This will include adopting a national health policy, as well as providing the appropriate range of services that meet the criteria for "availability, accessibility, acceptability, and quality" set out above. Special care is taken to point to neglected groups that often suffer from poor protection of human rights. These include women, children, older persons, indigenous people, and people with disabilities—indeed, virtually everyone who has limited access to the instruments of power within a society.

In terms of international obligations, as one would expect there are references to the obligation to provide economic and technical assistance, especially in the face of the gross health inequalities in the world, both within countries and between them. But this is not all. Just as states have the "duty to respect" and the "duty to protect," so does the international community. No state should take action that undermines the health of the people in other states; explicitly mentioned is that no state should impose embargoes on the supply of medicine or medical goods to another. Furthermore, states have the obligation to prevent third parties from taking steps that would undermine the right to health in other countries. Most importantly, there is an explicit reference to international financial organizations, especially the World Bank and the International Monetary Fund, which have been accused of insisting on economic policies that have weakened health systems and been detrimental to health in their client states. Even more expansively, the General Comment declares that there is a duty on states to provide humanitarian and disaster relief in emergencies to the limit of their capacities, and that while only states are parties to the international agreements, all people, organizations, and private companies also have responsibilities in respect of realizing the right to health.

These, then, are the duties to which the Committee on Economic, Social, and Cultural Rights considered states to be committed in order to realize the highest attainable standard of physical and mental health. But to what extent do countries follow these requirements? In a landmark article in *The Lancet* in 2008, Paul Hunt, then just ending his term as United Nations Special Rapporteur on the Human Right to Health, and colleagues attempted to provide a methodology to assess the degree to which different countries of the world could be said to be realizing the right to health. They surveyed 194 countries by means of seventy-two indicators.[29] One unsurprising finding was that, for many of the indicators, what they called "globally accessible" data was simply not available. Examples included whether the state undertook a health impact assessment before adopting its national health policy, and whether human rights training is a compulsory part of the curriculum for doctors or nurses. It is not that no country does this, but rather that no country makes it easy for people to find out. For some countries very little accessible data could be found, although those countries that have recently been the subject of WHO assistance often had more information available than wealthier countries.

The *Lancet* paper is a fascinating snapshot of the state of the realization of the right to health around the world, although methodologically, critics question whether the human right to health is clear enough to make it possible to monitor compliance. General Comment 14 is far from precise at the level of detail. Although some of the questions are obvious to ask in relation to health—life expectancy, per capita expenditure on medicine—it is unclear what the "correct" answer is. How much should expenditure be in order to be compliant? Other questions are much more procedural, such as whether the civil registration scheme of the country collects data disaggregated by sex, ethnic origin, rural or urban residence, socioeconomic status, or age. Other indicators address the determinants of health, such as access to clean water or the prevalence of violence against women, and indeed the survey starts rather bluntly by asking how many international treaties that recognize the right to health has the country ratified, and, secondly, whether the right to health has been recognized in domestic law.[30] What is particularly interesting for us in this chapter, however, is the emphasis on national health strategy and planning within the survey. Clearly the authors take the idea of progressive realization very seriously. While it would be unrealistic to think that many countries of the world are able to come close to full realization of the right to health, if indeed we can understand what that idea means, the survey is especially keen to monitor whether or not countries can be said to be making a serious attempt at progressive realization through the formulation of appropriate plans.[31]

Reading the *Lancet* report, one is struck by the immense effort that must have gone into producing the data it relies on. The human and other resources spent simply collecting figures, and, indeed, the underlying planning that is being monitored, may look like a huge bureaucratic exercise. Yet in noting this we see one of the paradoxes of large organizations. Everyone, it seems, is in favor of accountability. But accountability requires bureaucracy, and, it also seems, everyone is against that. Now, of course, although bureaucracy is necessary for accountability it is not sufficient: it will not guarantee accountability. However, collecting data—especially data disaggregated by age, gender, ethnicity, and social and economic status—can be hugely beneficial. First, it allows countries to monitor themselves, to see whether the resources they commit really do have the effect they intend, especially for the most disadvantaged groups. Second, it makes the health policy of a country visible to the international community, and, provided that the country cares about its reputation, may provide an incentive to change. Yet we have to be aware that, on the other hand, hitting targets can become an end in itself and undermine the quality it is intended to promote. There may be no easy way out of this dilemma, but at least under current circumstances monitoring countries against a wide range of targets probably has many more advantages than disadvantages.

THE HUMAN RIGHT
TO HEALTH IN PRACTICE

We have, so far in this chapter, looked primarily at conceptual and philosophical questions. A quite different argument focuses on what we might call the political sociology of human rights, and in particular rights of advocacy and empowerment. In recent decades, a good number of human rights organizations have come into being to protect the human rights of oppressed peoples. These include, of course, Amnesty International, now more than fifty years old, Human Rights Watch, and many others. Such organizations campaign, lobby, and take legal action on behalf of those whose rights have been violated. This, it is said, while often highly beneficial and effective, nevertheless has the effect of further disempowering disadvantaged people. Human rights activists will tend to be relatively privileged people from the developed world acting on behalf of others, who will be passive beneficiaries of their energetic activities.

Once more we must, I believe, admit that this is a real danger, and encourage NGOs to review their own role in possibly compounding the disempowerment of disadvantaged people. For this reason, some of the most encouraging developments in human rights activism are precisely those that facilitate disadvantaged people's self-advocacy, as we will explore later. The role for NGOs is to provide training and support, and to help form a radicalized and empowered community, able to fight its own battles in the future. It is therefore highly important for NGOs to focus not only on the goals of their campaigns, but the means by which those goals are obtained. It should be part of the mission statement of every development NGO that its ultimate aim is to make itself redundant, or at least regularly to review the reasons for its existence.

A more recent, and very urgent, criticism is that the practice of advocacy for the human right to health has done more harm than good. This argument has been made by William Easterly,[32] who is a very perceptive commentator on development issues and must be taken seriously.[33] Easterly's specific argument is that pressing for the right to health leads to distorted health priority-setting, diverting resources, effectively, to those who shout the loudest and are most effective in their advocacy, to the detriment of general health promotion. Easterly claims that pursuing the right to health leads to resources being spent in an inefficient manner, and that societies would be better off with cost-effective health-maximizing strategies.

There are at least two issues here. One is that a human rights culture favors those who have access, via lawyers, to the courts, namely the wealthy and well-connected.[34] The second is that human rights advocacy encourages interventions with a narrow focus, be it HIV/AIDS, malaria, maternal care or whatever. This, in turn, leads to what are called "vertical programs" that mobilize resources around a single condition, which can have the effect of severely weakening health systems.

Easterly is certainly right that single-issue advocacy can be damaging to health systems. For example, it has been argued that in sub-Saharan Africa, as ever more money is spent on HIV/AIDS programs, the proportion of attended births goes down.[35] The reason for this is that health workers are drawn to the better-funded campaign areas and away from general practice, which is left depleted of skilled personnel. This is a very serious problem which we will explore in detail in chapter 4.

However, it is unclear why Easterly should think that the problem of vertical programs is somehow intimately connected with the right to health. Advocacy for the human right to health is as likely to be addressed to health-system strengthening, including public health, as to single-issue projects, and, indeed, as the problem is becoming better known advocacy is increasingly focused on systems rather than particular diseases.

With respect to his other claim, that a human rights culture in effect diverts resources to the already wealthy and well-connected, the position is mixed. In chapter 3, we will see examples of jurisdictions, most notably South Africa, where judges have explicitly argued that courts of law are not the right fora for health resource allocation decisions to take place. In these jurisdictions there is no evidence that the human right to health has led to judicial decisions overturning cost-effective state decisions about health services. Although court action is the ultimate sanction for human rights abuse, in reality in many jurisdictions it is rare, while, as we saw in chapter 2, policies of "naming and shaming" are more common and effective,[36] and may be pursued in respect to the poor and vulnerable. Consider, for example, the study of "excess deaths" in the aftermath of the invasion of Iraq, which showed that the number of civilian deaths in Iraq after the invasion was much higher than normal, not only from death by violence, which suggests that the invasion led to a general increase in health problems and a reduced capacity to deal with them. Although not explicitly part of a human rights agenda, it is highly appropriate for that purpose.[37]

However, not all legal cultures act in the same way. In Latin America there have been very many—perhaps even tens of thousands—cases in which human right to health arguments have led to court orders for treatment, and in the great majority of examples for access to expensive medicines at public expense.

For example, it is claimed that in Brazil there is now an "epidemic of litigation" under the heading of the right to life and right to health, for access to therapies for not only HIV/AIDS but also for diabetes, Alzheimer's, and multiple sclerosis, among other conditions. The evidence appears to be that the successful litigants tend to come from socially and economically more advantaged groups.[38] How damaging this is overall is unclear, but it is a reasonable conjecture that it is damaging health equity and cost-effective planning. The lesson from Easterly's challenge is important. It should never complacently be assumed that attempts to do good can do no harm. This is as true for rights advocacy as it is for anything else.

The purpose of this chapter has been to examine two different ways in which the idea of the human right to health has come under pressure. One challenge worries about its moral foundations, the other its practical application and consequences. In the process of exploring the meaning, foundations and implications of the human right to health, we have also clarified its content, in the form of General Comment 14. At the same time we have acknowledged that not everyone will accept that the criticisms have been adequately answered. But it is now time to turn to the real world of health and human rights, to the individual and social manifestation of illness and disease, and how thinking of health in terms of a human right can help facilitate action to prevent, or at least reduce, suffering. We will do this by means of a detailed case study of a vital area of global health, the HIV/AIDS epidemic. We will examine how human right to health theory and action developed alongside the HIV/AIDS epidemic, first in the developed world, but now as part of a global response.

HUMAN
ALTH

THE AWAKENING OF THE HUMAN
RIGHT TO HEALTH

The story of activism about the human right to health is inextricably linked with the HIV/AIDS crisis. This is not to say that only HIV/AIDS engages the human right to health—far from it—or even that every aspect of HIV/AIDS is a matter of human rights. But nevertheless the narrative—the as yet far from complete narrative—of HIV/AIDS brings to light human rights issues at every turn. To name just the most obvious, these include: discrimination against "outsider" groups; the need to confront taboo subjects; the spread of the epidemic to the most vulnerable; the conflict between public safety and individual freedom of movement and action; implicit racism in responses to the global spread of HIV/AIDS; restricted access to very expensive patented medicines; the need to inform, educate, and change the sexual behavior of people, including teenagers;

the neglect of patient populations by their governments; alleged human rights abuses by international financial institutions; the role of "people's health movements"; the unintended consequences of treatment programs; and, as Jonathan Mann puts it, "the social determinants of vulnerability."[1]

At the start of the AIDS crisis, in 1981, the idea of the human right to health barely featured as part of the political or health agenda. But things have changed to a point where in 2003 Nelson Mandela could tell his audience, "AIDS is no longer a disease, it is human rights issue,"[2] and the theme of World AIDS Day 2010 was "Access to Treatment and Human Rights."[3]

HIV/AIDS became a human rights issue first of all through the agitation and action of the gay community in San Francisco and New York, who were especially concerned about discrimination against, and harsh treatment toward, people living with HIV. These early campaigns provided an impetus and a model for AIDS and human rights activism more widely in North America and Western Europe, and then throughout the globe, ultimately seeing health itself, and access to treatment, as human rights issues. This in turn led to the maturing of the idea of the human right to health, which is now used to advocate not only for treatment for all manner of diseases, but for the strengthening of health systems and for the provision of the underlying determinants of health, such as sanitation and nutrition. This chapter will explain how the fledgling idea of the human right to health developed, through AIDS activism, into a truly global concern.

Tragically, then, HIV/AIDS and the human right to health were made for each other. Our task in this chapter will be to look at the interlinked development of HIV/AIDS and the human right to health movement as a way of casting light on both. Jonathan Mann, one of the leading figures in making the connection between human rights and HIV/AIDS, very sadly a victim of the SwissAir crash of 1998, observed that "the human rights framework offers public health a more coherent, comprehensive and practical framework for analysis and action on the societal root causes of vulnerability to HIV/AIDS than any framework inherited from traditional public health or biomedical science."[4] But equally, HIV/AIDS gave the human right to health movement an impetus and a clear focus.

In this chapter we will explore, first, the response to HIV/AIDS in the developed world, and then widen the analysis to look at the global spread of HIV/AIDS, especially in Africa. Throughout we will consider those issues that are most salient from the point of view of the human right to health, and will draw the various strands together in the concluding section of the chapter.

HIV/AIDS DISCOVERY AND RESPONSE

The first cases of what came to be identified as HIV/AIDS emerged in the USA in 1981. In thinking through the immediate response to HIV/AIDS, it is important to remember that it arose at a time when it was thought that at least the developed world had passed through the "epidemiological transition" to a point where infectious disease had largely been conquered, and that the health challenges of the future would be chronic diseases of aging and lifestyle, especially heart disease and cancer. Although recent outbreaks of hepatitis and genital herpes had knocked the medical world's confidence to some degree, still no one was prepared to deal with a major new infectious disease. Nevertheless, once it switched into gear, the scientific response was remarkable.

The first identified patient groups, referred to at the time as the "four H's"—homosexuals, heroin users, hemophiliacs and Haitians,[5] sometimes accompanied by a fifth "H," hookers[6]— included, of course, groups who were already marginalized and stigmatized. Indeed, when first reported in June 1981, the condition was referred to as GRID: Gay Related Immune Deficiency, as all the members of the initial patient group were gay men who had acquired unusual infections and other rare conditions such as the cancer Kaposi's sarcoma as a result of a highly compromised immune system. AIDS was often referred to as "the gay plague," although, of course, other patient groups soon became known. The presence of injecting drug users and hemophiliacs indicated that the condition, whatever it was, must be transmissible through blood, whereas the presence of Haitians was, initially, more baffling, and led to wild speculation about voodoo and blood rituals.[7]

Even in the early 1980s we can detect connections between human rights and HIV/AIDS. Early speculation was that AIDS was the result of the promiscuous gay lifestyle of bathhouses and drugs. A type of moralistic "if they behave like that what do they expect?" led to popular support for severe restrictions on homosexual behavior, such as closure of bathhouses on public health grounds to prevent the further spread of the disease—not that it was known how it was spread. This was mixed in with genuine concern for those with the condition and their families, as well as a more matter-of-fact medical/scientific response underscored by a belief in a duty to understand and treat all conditions, whatever their cause. And, of course, there was greater sympathy for the hemophiliac patients, who were already in a perilous situation and could not have been thought to have brought their condition on themselves.

Stories about restriction, discrimination against "victims," and the protection of "the innocent" filled the media. Although in retrospect it is possible to describe some of the issues in terms of the right to health, to have done so at the time would have seemed a highly esoteric and exotic notion. Recall that the ESCR had only come into force, even among the countries that had ratified it, in 1976, and General Comment 14, offering detailed guidance on the right to health, was not issued until almost two decades later, in 2000. The US organization Physicians for Human Rights was not founded until 1986, and their focus, at least for some time, was on the health effects of civil and political rights abuse, such as torture, the death sentence, and inhumane prison conditions. Nevertheless, human rights issues were importantly engaged in another way: effectively, in the need to protect everyone's civil rights, such as freedom of movement and association, and freedom from prejudice and discrimination in the face of a virulent infection posing a deadly threat.

Jonathan Mann and colleagues helpfully distinguish three linkages between health and human rights. First, there are ways in which health policy can lead to human rights abuses, such as forced incarceration. Second, there are ways in which human rights abuses can have severely adverse health effects, as in the case of torture, but also in more mundane cases such as extreme poverty and discrimination in access to health services. And finally there are cases where the human right to health is itself directly at issue in terms of the right to treatment.[8]

As we have already seen, human rights are generally regarded as creating three types of duties for governments: to respect, to protect, and to fulfill. The first includes the call on government not to violate rights through state-directed forms of discrimination. The second calls on the government to protect people from the victimization and prejudice of other individuals and institutions. The third requires the government to ensure the provision of necessary resources to all and to put into place policies, legislation, and infrastructure to guarantee secure enjoyment of rights.

The early connection between human rights and health was primarily concerned with discrimination, exclusion, and protection. First, governments themselves had to decide how to treat individuals who had, or were believed to be at risk for, AIDS, given the seriousness of the condition. Traditional public health responses may have indicated forced isolation, for example. Should governments pursue this policy, or would it fail to respect the rights of people with AIDS? Would failure to do so be to fall down in the duty to protect the rights of other citizens, failing to protect them from a serious threat to health?

Second, how should the medical profession behave? As David Lush, an HIV activist living with HIV in Namibia points out, HIV "lays bare the myth of medical invincibility."[9] The medical profession was faced with a devastating condition for which it had no cure or, for a long time, any significant strategies for mitigation. The medical profession could, and did, treat secondary infections as they arose, but what should they do, for example, about informing patients of the doctor's assessment of their underlying condition? In the absence of any definitive test, they had to decide whether they should petrify the patient by revealing their suspicions, or paternalistically keep everything in a state of uncertainty or even false reassurance. Which policy would be more compliant with respecting human rights? And finally, governments had to formulate policies to deal with discrimination in housing, employment, insurance, and so on. Is it reasonable to allow individuals to choose who to associate with, and thereby exclude contact with those whom they believe to be infected with a fatal disease for which there is no cure, or is this unjustified discrimination?

Many of these questions could not be resolved until more was known about the condition and its modes of transmission. After initial speculative hypotheses about its causes, work in the USA and France led to a scientific consensus around 1983 that AIDS was caused by a previously unknown retrovirus, subsequently called HIV, and all known forms of transmission were through mixing of bodily fluids and especially blood contact. Once this was understood, it was not necessary to know the precise cause to be able to recommend and implement public health measures to reduce infection, such as safe sex, no sharing of needles among drug addicts, and much more rigorous handling of medical blood products especially for transfusion. Many of these precautions have now become a routine fact of life, such as sports players leaving the field to have cuts attended to, whereas once they would have heroically played on, or supermarkets selling condoms on open shelves, when once any such purchase would have been furtive and hidden. Having a more precise account of causation, however, generated the possibility of therapies. It was thought that it should be a relatively routine matter to develop a vaccine, just as medical research had done for other viral diseases such as smallpox, measles, mumps, rubella, polio, and influenza.[10] A huge research effort was set in motion, especially in the US.

One of the first practical discoveries, in 1984, was a blood test for HIV infection, which gave rise to the possibility of screening programs, and then acting on the basis of the information received. Interestingly, Peter Baldwin points out that although HIV/AIDS presented effectively the same problem throughout Western Europe as it did in North America, different countries took significantly different approaches.[11] The USA and Sweden, he argues, tended to take more restrictive measures than, for example, France and (with the exception of Bavaria) Germany, by undertaking such measures as closing their borders to immigrants who were HIV-positive, and, in some cases, even enforcing isolation. This may seem surprising, as the USA and Sweden have a reputation as the more liberal societies. Whether this liberal reputation is really deserved could be debated but Baldwin argues that every country already had in place a set of practices and regulations to deal with much earlier outbreaks of infectious disease, and their initial response was, for the most part, to dust off and roll out pre-existing policies. Public health measures could include isolation; a requirement to disclose HIV status to sexual partners; forced treatment; restrictions on who could enter the country or donate blood or breast milk; forced screening of risk groups (including pregnant women, prostitutes and their clients, prisoners, medical personnel, or even the whole population); contact tracing; registration and notification of change of address; restrictions on marriage; criminalization of, or assigning civil liability for, knowing or reckless transmission; compulsory sterilization of HIV-positive women or forced abortion; exclusion of children from school; and special regulations about the disposal of bodies after death.

Most of these strategies were attempted somewhere, as were many others, such as the regulation, in West Australia, that made it an offense "for a seropositive to board a public bus without notifying the driver."[12] In many places much turned on whether HIV/AIDS was to be classified as a sexually transmitted disease. A decision to do so was made in Sweden, which meant that those identified as HIV-positive were denied benefits available to those with other conditions, and in addition were subjected to very rigorous public health regulations, with dozens of people eventually subjected to forced isolation.[13] Interestingly, General Comment 14, which we considered in chapter 2, discusses the circumstances under which forced isolation is morally legitimate, suggesting that in addition to being carried out only when deemed strictly necessary, the least restrictive practice should be adopted, and it should be of limited duration and subject to review. In a later European Court judgment, Sweden was held to have violated the human right to liberty of the plaintiff, an HIV-positive man who was held in forced isolation, by adopting more restrictive measures than were necessary.[14]

It is also worth keeping in mind that the women most at risk—drug users and the partners of addicts—were, in the US, disproportionately black and Hispanic, and thus members of groups that historically had suffered sterilization and eugenic policies as well as much other discrimination. Hence, in the USA issues concerning reproduction and abortion were even more sensitive than they were elsewhere.[15]

While Sweden and the USA looked at measures to control the movement and activities of people with HIV/AIDS, especially imposing immigration and visiting restrictions on people with HIV, other countries put their emphasis on the education of people both with and without HIV/AIDS. It is widely noted that the policies actually adopted leaned either toward the authoritarian, enforcing preventative rules and regulations, or the consensual, where voluntary behavior change was taken to be key, with education, not enforcement, at the center. One of the best-known of the educational programs was the UK's "Don't Die of Ignorance" campaign of 1986–7, involving posters, leaflets, and TV advertising, suggesting, somewhat misleadingly, that the entire population was at risk for HIV infection.

With the medical profession relatively powerless to help, the research endeavor far from yielding a cure or, in the early days, effective mitigation, and governments slow to respond, it is not surprising that, as Peter Piot and colleagues note, civil society advocacy took the lead.[16] And, we should add, it was a recently radicalized and empowered, not to say reasonably affluent, section of civil society that did this. AIDS struck barely more than a decade after New York's Stonewall riots, often regarded as the start of the gay rights movement. Indeed, even until the early 1970s homosexuality had been considered an illness in the USA.[17] In the intervening years gay rights and gay pride groups had mobilized to fight against discrimination. With the advent of AIDS, much of this energy was channeled toward new organizations focused on the health of gay and bisexual men: promoting safer sexual practices and supporting those people who were living with AIDS, both medically and in terms of civil and political rights. Such groups included, in the USA, Gay Men's Health Crisis and San Francisco AIDS Foundation; in the UK, the Terrence Higgins Trust; and in France, AIDES, founded by Daniel Defert, the partner of philosopher Michel Foucault, who had died of AIDS in 1984.[18]

These civil society groups responded with impressive pace and force. A statement as early as 1983 when no treatment was available and "a diagnosis of AIDS was a death sentence," kicked back at the prejudice that was gripping Western societies. Set out by the Advisory Committee of People with AIDS, it became known as the Denver Principles, and although not written in the language of human rights is a striking model of what a comprehensive human rights charter might be for a group particularly at risk for a dangerous infectious disease. It begins with a powerful statement about classification:

> We condemn attempts to label us as "victims," a term which
> implies defeat, and we are only occasionally "patients," a term

which implies passivity, helplessness, and dependence upon the care of others. We are "People With AIDS."

It then moves on to recommendations for health care professionals, and then "recommendations for all people," "recommendations for people with AIDS," and finally "rights of people with AIDS." These latter sections are worth quoting at length:

RECOMMENDATIONS FOR ALL PEOPLE

1. Support & Membership in our struggle against those who would fire us from our jobs, evict us from our homes, refuse to touch us or separate us from our loved ones, our community or our peers, since available evidence does not support the view that AIDS can be spread by casual, social contact.

2. Not scapegoat people with AIDS, blame us for the epidemic or generalize about our lifestyles.

RECOMMENDATIONS FOR PEOPLE WITH AIDS

1. Form caucuses to choose their own representatives, to deal with the media, to choose their own agenda and to plan their own strategies.

2. Be involved at every level of decision-making and specifically serve on the board of directors of provider organizations.

3. Be included in all AIDS forums with equal credibility as other participants, to share their own experiences and knowledge.

4. Substitute low-risk sexual behaviors for those which could endanger themselves or their partners; we feel that people with AIDS have an ethical responsibility to inform their potential partners of their health status.

RIGHTS OF PEOPLE WITH AIDS

1. To live as full and satisfying sexual and emotional lives as anyone else.

2. To receive quality medical treatment and quality social service provision without discrimination of any form, including sexual orientation, gender, diagnosis, economic status or race.

3. To obtain full explanations of all medical procedures and risks, to choose or refuse their treatment modalities, to refuse to participate in research without jeopardizing their treatment and to make informed decisions about their lives.

4. To ensure privacy and confidentiality of medical records, to receive human respect and the right to choose who their significant others are.

5. To die—and to LIVE—in dignity.[19]

It is worth noting that the responsibilities of people with AIDS are not said to be to refrain from sex, as conservative approaches had advocated as in earlier decades regarding sexually transmitted disease, but to find safer forms of sex. This reflects a shift in outlook, in which, as Peter Baldwin puts it, "[Sex] was no longer regarded just as pleasure, much less as merely a happy interlude on the road to reproduction, but was also seen as a fundamental human right."[20]

The Denver Principles no doubt influenced the process leading to the much later "GIPA Principle"—Greater Involvement of People Living with HIV/AIDS—agreed at the 1994 Paris Aids Summit, which calls for the creation of supportive political, legal and social environments for people living with HIV/AIDS.[21] As a multinational agreement, rather than the mission statement of an activist group, inevitably the GIPA Principle lacks the punch of the Denver Principles, but nevertheless it implicitly acknowledged that health has complex social and political aspects and is not simply a matter for the medical profession.

The difficulty of responding to the AIDS crisis was well summed up by Australian judge Justice Michael Kirby, who warned against a class of new viruses: HIL, or Highly Inefficient Laws, by which he meant panicky and punitive restrictions on people with or at risk for HIV. Kirby argues that in general many laws are much less effective in changing behavior than we might naively suppose, and this is particularly likely to be the case regarding laws attempting to regulate the behavior of people with AIDS. As he puts it, some people's "physiological needs (whether for drugs or sex) are more powerful than their fears of detection and punishment."[22] In particular, he argued against forms of mandatory testing and certification, which, he suggests, are enormously costly for society and for the individuals tested, yet will have only the most marginal benefit, especially at a time when no cure or effective therapy is known. To give a sense of the cost–benefit analysis, consider the state of Illinois, which required premarital screening. In the first six months of the program 70,000 applicants were screened, at a cost of $2.5 million (charged to the applicants), but just eight people were found to be seropositive. And those who didn't want to be tested simply got married elsewhere.[23]

It might be thought that detecting eight people with HIV is a significant result and well worth the cost and inconvenience of the screening program. But to underscore Kirby's point, it is particularly important to note that the virus can be present in the body for some time before it creates antibodies. As the test detects not the virus itself but antibodies, it is likely to produce a significant number of false negatives of people who are relatively recently infected. For this reason mass screening could, in fact, be a threat to public health if infected individuals believe they have received the all-clear.

In essence, the early stages of the HIV/AIDS crisis brings into sharpest possible focus the central dilemma of human rights and public health in the face of infectious disease. How do you respect the human right to liberty of people living with the condition while protecting the human right to health of the much wider population who do not (yet) have it? In the history of infectious disease, it has been common to sacrifice the human rights of the ill, especially through enforced isolation, to protect the healthy.[24] However, there are hidden complexities in this argument, even beyond the question of balancing one set of rights against another. For in the mid- to late 1980s it was realized that unless the civil rights of people living with HIV/AIDS were protected, public health was at risk. People would not take tests if they feared that a positive result might be released or leaked to family, neighbors, employers, or insurers. This led, according to Jonathan Mann, for the first time, to the game-changing idea that preventing discrimination must be intrinsic to public health programs, as well as to a recognition that weak support for human rights for sex workers, illegal immigrants, the poor, drug addicts, and young homeless people itself became a risk factor for HIV infection.[25] Like many infectious diseases, HIV/AIDS started among the affluent and well-traveled, but before long gravitated toward those who are otherwise marginalized in society.

But unless we wish to argue, implausibly, that restrictive measures are always ineffective, there may be some policies that are both restrictive and effective in reducing the spread of disease, such as, perhaps, quarantine, as practiced in a relatively humane form in Cuba.[26] In the absence of knowledge of cause or cure, there is no obvious answer to what should be done. It would be no surprise to find exactly what Peter Baldwin has documented: that at least in the first decade, different countries or regions attempted to settle the balance in quite different ways, simply using the strategy they had always used in public health emergencies. But when the message sunk in that restricting the activities of people living with HIV simply made them less likely to come forward, a consensus settled on respecting their human rights to liberty and non-discrimination.[27]

ACCESS TO TREATMENT

There was a period, we have seen, in which HIV/AIDS could be detected by blood test but no therapy was available. Under such circumstances, the human right to health of those infected has little or no application.[28] Fortunately, initial scientific progress was very rapid, with the first anti-retroviral treatment becoming available in 1987. This was the previously known but clinically unused drug AZT (full name Azidothymidine, also known as Zidovudine and Retrovir) which had been designed as a cancer treatment. AZT was found to be effective in the test tube against HIV in 1985, and after an unusually rapid development through clinical trial, came into general use just two years later. This speed was remarkable, for the research ethics of testing what might be the first treatment of a fatal condition are exceptionally tense. To test efficacy it is standard scientific practice to use a randomized control trial, in which one group is given the active drug and the other a placebo. Such a trial was conducted and the results, published in 1987, were encouraging. A total of 282 patients took part and were given treatment for between eight and twenty-four weeks. By the end of treatment nineteen patients in the control arm had died but only one who received

AZT.[29] However, serious side effects were observed, to the point where some had to stop treatment.[30]

The sample size was small, and although the trial was highly promising normally much more research would be conducted before a drug was declared safe and effective enough to use. No doubt if the condition had not been so serious and politically highly charged, many more studies would have been conducted before release. But in this case, the ethical questions are very difficult. Is it acceptable to sign people up to a trial of this sort, people who are desperate for a cure and agree to be a subject of research in the hope that they might benefit, and then to assign them to the control arm to receive a placebo? Indeed, it could be thought a contravention of one's human rights to be assigned to the control arm, to be treated as a means toward scientific progress.

In addition, before a drug is released it is normally subjected to safety tests to determine whether it has side effects. But if it is effective against a fatal threat, we might wonder whether to care about the side effects. Isn't it a violation of people's right to health to delay releasing the treatment while the side effects are tested? As it turned out, the sense of crisis meant that it was almost inevitable that the humanitarian arguments would win out over the "sound science" arguments, with questions of the rights of research subjects apparently submerged in the urgency of the situation. Arguably, this left the medical establishment later vulnerable to accusations that the new therapies had never been fully tested.

Once AZT became available, it was used at first as a treatment to mitigate the development of HIV/AIDS, reducing the viral load, but by 1990 it was understood that it could be used as a preventive measure as well, in particular to prevent mother-to-child transmission. But there remained an underbelly of HIV skepticism, led by University of California, Berkeley biologist Peter Duesberg and others, which denied that HIV was the cause of AIDS. If correct this would have meant that AZT was useless, even counterproductive. Indeed, there were arguments that the main symptoms of AIDS were actually caused by the toxic effects of AZT. When it was first introduced, AZT was used in what are now regarded as very high doses and the side effects were often severe. In any case, treatment increased survival only for a matter of months rather than years. Even the medical establishment had to concede that AZT was by no means a cure, even though it did extend life.[31]

This radical skepticism overlapped with a legitimate set of general concerns over the effectiveness and serious side effects of medications—the phenomenon of iatrogenic disease (physician-induced illness)—as well as the general sociological issues of "medicalization." Those regarded as suffering from serious illness can find their life taken over by the medical profession to a point where they become a "victim" of a disease or "patient" in the sense we saw the Denver Principles trying to resist, rather than a person who happens to be living with a condition. These concerns, we can see, intersect with human rights in that one's life can be taken over by the medical profession, destroying the dignity and sense of control of the individual. It is entirely reasonable to try to resist medicalization, but in this case resistance sometimes took the form of objection to medication, which was particularly tragic when much more effective medication later did become available.

Questioning whether the treatment is effective is one thing. Who should pay for it is another, and here the human right to health takes on a new dimension: the human right to access to treatment. These issues were more straightforward in some countries than others. Where there is a national health system, the right to health has already been embedded in national priorities, and once a treatment becomes available for prescription, all who qualify, as in Britain and Sweden, received treatment without charge. More difficult was whether this should be extended to recent immigrants, especially those known to be HIV-positive on arrival. Countries with universal coverage funded by tax or national insurance had standard procedures already in place, although it appears that in some cases, such as in France, members of highly excluded groups, such as drug addicts and illegal immigrants, fell through the cracks in the system and remained uninsured and untreated. And, of course, these are high-risk groups for HIV/AIDS.[32] The system in the USA, however, was not well-equipped to supply expensive treatments to a vulnerable population. In the 1980s, when AZT was available but only at high cost, many people with HIV lacked coverage, others lost coverage when they were no longer able to work, and still others found their insurance not covering many of the costs, or even being terminated. Medicaid could cover some of these people, but not the "working poor" or those with savings, and so it became common for people to "asset-strip" to qualify for government assistance.

After pressure and the recognition that the situation in the US was unacceptable and unsustainable, a new law, the Ryan White Comprehensive AIDS Resources Emergency Act (CARE), was passed in 1990. Ryan White was a teenage hemophiliac who had been subject to vicious discrimination in his home town after being diagnosed with AIDS; later, his family moved to a much more receptive and welcoming district, and the publicity concerning his plight led to his being befriended by celebrities such as Elton John and Michael Jackson. This in turn created greater publicity and he became a celebrity himself, often appearing on television to talk about his life and experiences. Elton John was present at his deathbed and played the piano at his funeral.[33] It is said that the national attention to his case—an ordinary American boy who was neither homosexual nor a drug user, but happened to become infected through blood products—helped normalize HIV/AIDS in the USA, alongside diagnoses of celebrities such as movie star Rock Hudson, tennis player Arthur Ashe, and basketball player Magic Johnson. Ryan White died in 1990, and in that year the CARE Act was passed in his name. It provides medical care as a last resort, when all other avenues of funding are exhausted or not available. It is an example of what is often called "AIDS exceptionalism" for, apart from the anomalous example of renal dialysis,[34] it is only in the case of HIV/AIDS that the USA guarantees paid medical care for all. Other laws were also passed in the USA to ensure continuity of insurance, such as the Consolidated Omnibus Budget Reconciliation Act of 1986 (COBRA), which allowed people leaving employment to maintain their workplace health insurance for a fixed period.[35] In retrospect we can see these measures as an implicit recognition of the human right to health, in the sense of the right to access to treatment. It would simply be a gross offence against human dignity to allow the citizens of a wealthy country to die when drugs to extend their lives are available and are being used by many of their fellow citizens who happen to have the wealth or the right health plan.

Access to therapy, and in particular AZT, became close to universal in the developed world. However, we have seen already that AZT is not particularly effective. One reason for this is that HIV rapidly mutates in the human body. Not only this, but the HIV virus imprints itself within human chromosomes, so that once infection has occurred it seems impossible to remove.[36] Rapid mutation makes a vaccine very difficult to develop—much more so than was optimistically assumed at first—and it also means that the virus can easily become resistant to drugs. For this reason AZT became used as part of combination therapies in the 1990s using several different drugs together—"triple therapy"—to combat resistance. Finally, in the mid-1990s a new type of drug became available, known as protease inhibitors, and in combination with AZT or similar drugs treatment proved much more effective. This treatment is known as HAART (highly active anti-retroviral therapy). By use of such approaches HIV is now regarded in wealthy countries as more akin to a chronic illness, such as diabetes, requiring regular medication, rather than the immediate death sentence it once seemed to be. This is not to say that there are no ethical or policy questions still in need of attention. The major issue, of course, is the very high cost of HAART and who should pay for it. In the UK, for example, it is estimated that the annual cost is £16,000 (although it seems that some doctors do not have the budget to prescribe the most expensive new therapies). Despite the expense, the price paid is sometimes said to be very cost-effective as it keeps people living with HIV from opportunistic infections which would be much more expensive to treat, as well as allowing them to function as productive members of society.[37]

Where, then, are we regarding the human right to health and HIV/AIDS in the wealthy countries? If we think of the human right to health as offering protection from "standard threats to health," then HIV/AIDS is now a standard threat and we have the means, both technical and financial, to meet that threat, and a range of laws and institutions in place to make doing so almost a matter of medical routine. Discrimination in the workplace and housing is now largely a thing of the past, partly as a result of highly active human rights campaigns: first, campaigns against discrimination and victimization in all its forms, and second, campaigns for the right to treatment.

In sum, in wealthy countries governments have made a great deal of progress in meeting their requirements to respect, protect, and fulfill the human right to health, at least in respect to HIV/AIDS. But they did not do this unprompted. Grassroots protest and action pressured governments to protect the rights and civil liberties of people living with HIV, and to engage in public health campaigns for the sake of the general population. Campaigning groups forced the hand of government to sponsor research and to find ways to subsidize expensive treatments.

Yet this is not the whole picture. We noted above that HIV/AIDS, like all infectious diseases, eventually seeks out the marginalized, wherever it starts. People of disadvantaged status, such as those illegally resident in the country, the homeless, drug addicts, and prostitutes, are now at much higher risk than the rest of the population, and do not always receive access to diagnosis and medication. Writing in 1992, Paul Farmer noted, "Among young black women living in New York State AIDS has recently become the leading cause of death."[38] "Hard-to-reach" groups remain relatively neglected even now, and so there is human right to health work still to be done, even in the wealthiest countries of the world.

HIV/AIDS AND HAITIANS
IN THE UNITED STATES

As we saw, Haitians were identified as one of the "four H's"; the early risk groups for AIDS before HIV was identified. Being singled out in such a way gave rise, immediately, to speculation about voodoo practices involving blood—speculation not only in the popular press, but in respected medical journals.[39] Equally, discussion focused on the possibility that although open homosexuality was very rare in Haiti, the country nevertheless must have functioned as a destination for gay American sex tourists. This then raised the further question of direction of travel. Did the USA inadvertently import AIDS from Haiti, or was it spread in the other direction? Indeed, did both countries receive their first infections from other sources? Doubts, speculations, and uncertainties draw out several issues of great importance for thinking about human rights and health.

Before looking in more detail at HIV/AIDS in Haitians in the United States, it is worth providing just a little background about Haiti itself. Propelled into the world media by the tragic earthquake of 2010 which killed perhaps a quarter of a million people and left hundreds of thousands still without homes or even adequate shelter as I write more than a year later, Haiti was already known as the poorest country in the western hemisphere, with shocking rates of illiteracy and child mortality, as well as many other indicators of desperate poverty. It is around 700 miles from Florida—hence accessible by an often perilous boat journey—and 50 miles east of Cuba. It occupies the western portion of the island evocatively called Hispaniola, the eastern part of which forms the Dominican Republic. Haiti gained independence from its colonial master, France, in 1804, by means of a slave rebellion that had taken more than a decade of violent struggle.[40] It has never prospered. First, it was subjected to ruinous compensation payments to France, agreed in 1825 as a condition of France's recognition of Haiti's independence. It is also troubled by constant interference in its affairs by its dominant and bullying northern neighbor, which was at first especially worried, in the Southern slave states, by the example set of a slave rebellion. International trade and cooperation was problematic throughout the nineteenth century, with foreign business interests increasingly intervening in Haitian politics and an unsustainable national debt accumulating.

The US invaded Haiti in 1915 as the culmination of an increasingly interventionist stance over the previous decades, and ultimately took full control, instituting a new constitution which for the first time allowed foreign ownership of land, a policy that was aggressively pursued. Karl Marx pointed out that in late feudal England, the dispossession of the peasantry led to a supply of ready—desperate and therefore cheap—labor. These comments could equally be applied to Haiti, which became a cheap labor source supplying the American market. François Duvalier (Papa Doc) was elected president in 1957, but over the following years converted his popular rule into an increasingly corrupt and repressive dictatorship, enforced by the brutal Tonton Macoutes. On his death in 1971 he was replaced by his nineteen-year-old son Jean-Claude (Baby Doc) who continued in power until 1985. Over this period Haiti remained essentially a subcontracting outpost for the United States. It was also heavily dependent on overseas aid, much of it in the form of loans, which turned it into one of the most heavily indebted countries in the world. An astonishing portion of this aid was siphoned off into the Swiss bank accounts of the Duvaliers and their associates.

A popular revolt in 1986 brought down the Duvalier family. Then followed a period of great instability punctuated by several coups d'état and politically motivated massacres.[41] Finally, in 1990, Haiti had a genuinely democratic election, and voted Jean-Bertrand Aristide president. Unfortunately, 1991 saw another military coup that lasted until 1994 when Aristide was restored to power. Following the example of Costa Rica, he put in place steps to disband the army, but that was not enough to prevent yet another military coup in 2004, this time widely believed to have been financed and organized by the USA, and indirectly prompted by an aid embargo designed to force Aristide into political reforms, which left Haiti unable to rise above its grinding poverty.

As a result of the appalling conditions at home, many Haitians sought a life elsewhere, hundreds of thousands emigrating to North America. There, though, they often suffered routine discrimination. The revelation that Haitians were especially at risk for AIDS was a further blow to their standing in North American society, and instantly gave rise to the speculation that AIDS must have arrived in the USA from Haiti.

This question of causal direction has been hotly debated. In 1992, Paul Farmer wrote, "What data exist do not support the thesis that HIV reached North America from Haiti,"[42] and he advanced the thesis that HIV had reached Haiti through American sex tourists, and then spread through heterosexual contact, especially to the poor and vulnerable who moved to the city as their best hope of survival. His case studies are consistent with this view, as is his finding that a very high prevalence rate was to be found in the Port-au-Prince suburb of Carrefour, which was the main center of both female and male prostitution in Haiti. However, in 2007 research was published, based on analysis of the HIV virus and its subtypes, suggesting that the HIV-1 B virus, which is the most prevalent form of the virus outside Southern Africa and India (where in both regions HIV-1 C is dominant), moved from Africa to Haiti some time in the late 1960s. It appears that the virus stayed within Haiti for several years, transmitted largely through heterosexual contact, before being dispersed more broadly, including into the USA, where, according to this analysis, it arrived in about 1969, through a single transmission.[43]

Does it matter? The question of origin is of historical interest, but more importantly perhaps, it is vital in the attempt to design vaccines. Knowing which are the earliest forms of the virus, and how they transfer and mutate, will be necessary if a universally effective vaccine is ever to be produced. It is less clear, however, that there is any immediate ethical significance in these findings. Many Americans wanted to "blame" Haiti for AIDS; others wanted to blame North Americans for bringing AIDS to Haiti. With regard to this dispute, moral philosophers will point out that commentators have failed to distinguish causal responsibility and moral responsibility. An avalanche may be triggered by a mountaineer's cough. Although causally responsible he or she is unlikely to be morally responsible, unless it was already known that an avalanche was a real possibility and coughing a real risk. In the case of HIV/AIDS, no one could have known that their behavior had any real probability of leading to a pandemic. The notion of moral blame is out of place, whichever way the virus was transmitted (unless, of course, one of the wild conspiracy theories turns out to be correct). Once the virus was in the human population, some or other route of transmission was very likely. Nevertheless, it must be acknowledged that such academic moral arguments, however strong, are unlikely to undercut public attributions of blame, for which causal history is central. But we should note that all sides in this debate, heatedly trying to assert or deny a causal pathway, run the risk of making the same confusion between causal and moral responsibility.

There could well, though, be public health implications of knowing the origin of the condition. If it is true that HIV/AIDS had been circulating in Haiti before it arrived in the USA, it is likely that the prevalence among Haitians would be higher than that of the citizens of the USA, and therefore, from a purely medical perspective, it would be reasonable to treat Haitians as a special risk group, as, indeed, was done without solid evidence when AIDS was first identified.

Yet what follows, at an official level, from being identified as a member of a high-risk group is another matter. It could be, for example, that members of a special risk group could be offered additional help. Alternatively, their activity could be restricted, as happened in various times and in various ways. Again we see the central human rights dilemma: is it right to restrict the liberty of one group in order to protect the health of another? Many will instead argue for a consensual approach: encourage those giving blood to understand the issues and not to donate if they have any doubts. The problem is that even if a measure is indicated from a medical point of view, medicine does not operate in a socially sterile environment. Public-health ordinances can create considerable damage, most obviously of stigma, but, as we will see, much deeper than that.

In the USA, unfortunately, quite often a heavy hand was tried first, and even if policy changed later, irreparable damage had been done. Once Haitians were identified as a risk category the further consequences were devastating. For one thing, the Haitian tourist industry, which had been a major source of foreign revenues and employment, collapsed, with Americans no longer willing to risk setting foot on the island. For Haitians living in the USA, a group already struggling for being "black, foreign, and French/Creole speaking"[44] the association between their country of origin and AIDS led to a whole gamut of discrimination and prejudice, from playground taunts to bankruptcy of small business owners and eviction. It is reported that many Haitians learned to pass themselves off as from other French-speaking Caribbean islands.[45]

In response to pressure and lobbying, the New York City Department of Health removed Haitians from their list of risk groups in 1983. As Paul Farmer notes, "The category was not easily removed, however, from the list then firmly implanted in the popular imagination."[46] It took a further two years for the Centers for Disease Control (CDC) to follow suit, but even this gave Haitians little relief.

Further damage to Haitians was done offstage. In the narrative of HIV/AIDS, it is the coup of 1991 that is the key moment in the story. Aristide had a great deal of popular support, and thus the military coup that ousted him was widely opposed. Once the military had taken power it started to arrest and execute Aristide's supporters. Fearing for their lives many took flight, especially over water to the USA, where they became known as "boat people." This was not new. Large numbers of Haitians had sought refuge in the USA for the preceding decades, but an agreement between the USA and Haiti meant that almost all of them were returned. Paul Farmer cites the astonishing statistic that between 1981 and 1991, 24,559 Haitian refugees sought asylum in the USA, and just eight were accepted.[47] For a short time after the military coup of 1991 the USA suspended this policy, but then, against the protests of humanitarian organizations and the United Nations, reinstated it again.

Then the USA agreed to a compromise. Instead of returning the refugees to Haiti and a highly uncertain future, they would be sent to a place of safety: chillingly, to the now notorious Guantánamo Bay, a US military base on the island of Cuba. Although represented as a "haven" or "oasis" for Haitians, it was more like an internment camp. Here, in their thousands, they were housed in tents and temporary shelters in a secure encampment for months, unable to leave, and some complaining of severe mistreatment by the American military personnel. By summer 1992, Guantánamo was too overcrowded to accept any more refugees, so the policy changed again. Now Haitian refugees arriving by boat were to be returned to Haiti, in contrast with Cubans, all of whom were declared political refugees on arrival in the USA.

The USA did accept that some refugees were genuinely in danger of their lives. Paul Farmer tells the story of Yolande Jean, who managed to retain documents proving that she had previously been arrested and tortured. US law should have granted her a safe haven as a political refugee, and should have allowed her to be admitted after her assessment at Guantánamo. Unfortunately, as part of the process she was tested and found to be HIV-positive. By this time the USA had adopted the highly restrictive policy of denying those who were HIV-positive entry into the country. This policy was adopted for two reasons: one was the risk to public health, the other that the USA was not prepared to pay for treatment for new immigrants.[48] Yolande Jean was not returned to Haiti, but instead kept at Guantánamo as one of around 200 HIV-positive Haitians who had a genuine case for asylum. They were housed close together under conditions in which they were likely to pass on to each other opportunistic infections such as tuberculosis. Although the camp was represented as a medical facility, it had few medical staff. Demonstrations and protests brought only harsher treatment, and Yolande Jean led a hunger strike, which, according to her report, was dealt with by brutal beatings. Some inmates attempted to escape, others to commit suicide. Eventually, in 1993 Judge Johnson declared the camp illegal and the refugees, including Yolande Jean, were admitted to the USA. The judge noted that it was "the only known refugee camp in the world composed entirely of HIV-positive refugees" given "the kind of indefinite detention usually reserved for spies and murderers."[49] Or, in the light of more recent history, one might add, those suspected of terrorism.

Once again we see the pointed clash between the human rights of those infected with HIV/AIDS and the right to health of those who are not infected. In this case, however, the clash is compounded by the fact that the health of those infected was largely neglected, and the threat posed to ordinary Americans by Haitian immigrants was negligible. But it took several years for these factors to bubble to the surface in a way that eventually led to a reasonable resolution.

THE GLOBAL SPREAD OF HIV/AIDS: AFRICA

By 1988, 138 countries had reported at least one case of HIV/AIDS to the World Health Organization, and by 2004 there were believed to be almost 40 million cases.[50] HIV/AIDS spread through South and South-East Asia, through Eastern Europe and through Latin America. But its presence has been felt most dramatically in sub-Saharan Africa.

Though it was discovered first in the USA, within a few years scientists were sure that HIV/AIDS had originated in Africa. Current theory is that the virus crossed the species barrier at least three times, in west central Africa. It is thought that the virus originated in chimpanzees and may have been transmitted to human beings, probably through the mixing of blood during the violence of hunting, twice directly from chimpanzees and once via gorillas,[51] although other primates such as the sooty mangabey are also mentioned.[52] The date of earliest crossover has been pushed further and further back and now some time at least before 1921 and perhaps even before 1902 is being suggested.[53] Accordingly, mysterious earlier deaths have been reexamined[54] and confirmed cases include a Norwegian sailor who, along with his wife and child, was infected; all died in 1976.[55]

Although HIV/AIDS infection in Africa was well-known, response was very slow, at least relative to the pace in the developed world. A combination of factors was responsible. For one thing, African governments, in some cases, were in no mood to publicize the existence of AIDS in their country, given that its best known means of transmission were injecting drugs and homosexual sex, both of which were even greater taboos and sources of shame in many African countries than in the wealthy nations.[56] Indeed, active discrimination against homosexuals remains common in many African countries. For example, homosexuality is illegal in Uganda, where a highly punitive anti-homosexuality bill was recently proposed.[57]

A second complicating factor was that there are two main strains of HIV: HIV-1 and HIV-2. HIV-1 is the source of the great majority of infections in the USA and Europe, but, initially at least, HIV-2 was more common in West Africa. The course of HIV-2 is slower than HIV-1, although eventually it has the same outcomes.[58] However, the existence of HIV-2 in West Africa gave rise to a belief that HIV infection in Africa generally was less serious than in the developed world, that it must have been around for some time without causing a major problem, and that it would not cause the deaths seen elsewhere. In truth, this may have been a comforting rationalization of inaction, mixed in with unconscious racism and the belief that life in Africa is "cheap" when there is so much early death in any case. Inaction, at least at first, was only to be expected (which is not to say justified) when the costs of action in the form of a wide public health response and, especially, highly expensive anti-retroviral treatment would have been enormous. However, one important difference between HIV/AIDS in Africa and the developed world was simply that in Africa it spread predominantly through heterosexual sex, and from the start a much higher proportion of women were infected. More than 50 percent of people living with HIV in sub-Saharan Africa are women.[59]

HIV is thought to have originated in western equatorial Africa, spread west to the Ivory Coast and east to the Democratic Republic of Congo (formerly Zaire) and then radiated through central Africa along rivers and trade routes. By the early 1980s AIDS was obviously present in Tanzania and in Uganda, where the symptoms of persistent untreatable diarrhea and subsequent weight loss led to it being referred to as "slim disease."[60] When reading medical papers, the technical names of conditions can have a numbing and abstracting effect, so that one forgets what it is like for people, especially in poor resource settings, to suffer. Here is one moving description from the former Secretary-General of the International AIDS Society, L. O. Kallings:

> Previously strong and beautiful young people shrink to gnomes, in poor countries often lying unattended on the floor with fever, coughing due to tuberculosis or pneumonia or other causes, constant diarrhoea and difficulty in eating and drinking due to the pain caused by oral and oesophageal candidiasis. The skin is often affected with large shingle sores. People with AIDS are often very weak due to the deep asthenia, sometimes demented, sometimes blind due to cytomegalo-retinitis. They are totally helpless, often abandoned by any remaining family members or chased away to the outskirts of the village by neighbours who are afraid of contracting AIDS. Reportedly, people with AIDS may even be buried alive.[61]

AIDS spread through central Africa but concentrations were highest in Uganda and Tanzania. Infection spread into Zambia and Zimbabwe, but at first, during the apartheid era, South

Africa remained relatively little touched. With the end of apart-heid and the opening of the borders in 1994, the return of South Africans from exile and mass movement of labor, the picture changed dramatically and South Africa became the epicenter of the epidemic. It is true that Botswana and Swaziland had higher rates of infection, but South Africa has a much larger population. It is estimated that around 5 million people in South Africa are living with HIV and 600,000 have full-blown AIDS, with hundreds dying every day.[62] In addition to everything else AIDS is also a cause of severe financial difficulty, not just in terms of loss of wage-earners but because of the African tradi-tion of holding elaborate and very expensive funerals.[63]

Just as HIV/AIDS was taking a grip, development econom-ics turned in what would prove to be a catastrophic direction. The World Bank tied overseas aid and loans to "structural adjustment," attempting to bring developing countries out of poverty by stimulating the private sector and reducing the size and expenditure of the state, including public spending on the health sector. Whether or not this was the right thing to do from an economic point of view—and the results have not been encouraging—from the point of view of health it was a disas-ter, especially for countries trying to deal with the HIV/AIDS pandemic. It has been argued that the restrictions on health spending required by the World Bank and the International Monetary Fund left developing countries unable to meet their core obligations regarding the right to health of their citizens.[64]

At the same time that countries were unable to support their citizens' health needs and rights from their own resources, other international organizations came to begin to understand their obligations of assistance, although it took some time to crank into gear. The Global Program on AIDS was set up in 1987, with Jonathan Mann appointed as director. From the start

Mann emphasized the human rights of people living with HIV, arguing against forms of discrimination and punitive measures which would make things worse. Although it did a valuable job in raising awareness, lack of political and donor support limited the effectiveness of the Global Program.[65] In 1996, UNAIDS was founded with Peter Piot at its head, drawing together a number of different agencies and providing leadership and governance. But it was not until 2001 with the establishment of the Global Fund to Fight AIDS, Tuberculosis, and Malaria, that substantial funding was achieved. At this time United Nations Secretary-General Kofi Annan noted that life-saving medicines were out of financial reach of 90 percent of sufferers, and called for a war chest of $7–10 billion to meet the funding gap.

Some were skeptical. The cost of the drugs seemed to make the idea of mass programs utopian. But that was not all. Notoriously, in 2001 Andrew Natsios, head of USAID, argued that Africans lacked the concept of Western time and would not be able to keep to the rigorous drug regimen necessary for HAART, which would then lead to greater drug resistance and bigger problems in future if medication was attempted.[66] Equally it was said that HAART could only be administered in technically advanced systems where patients could be monitored, and to attempt to introduce it in other settings was worse than futile, for it would lead to the development of drug resistance.

Médecins Sans Frontières refused to accept this pessimism and set up some model treatment programs in the most difficult places, involving the use of relatively cheap generically manufactured drugs combining several therapies into a single pill and thereby reducing the complexity of treatment. They found other ways around high-tech monitoring and in 2003 were able to report adherence and survival rates comparable to those in the United States.[67] The skeptics were wrong-footed. People in the developing world could benefit from advanced treatment if it was made available to them, and the human right to health demanded that it should be. Arguably this was the period in which the human right to health movement came of age. As we noted at the start of this chapter, 2003 was the year Nelson Mandela declared that AIDS was no longer merely a disease but a human rights issue, and the same year the World Health Organization launched its "3 x 5" initiative, aiming to have 3 million people in anti-retroviral treatment by 2005. The target was missed, but nevertheless the initiative led to a huge scaling-up of effort.[68] It was not, though, until 2006 that the United Nations agreed to make universal access to treatment, prevention, care, and support its goal.[69] Money became available, with important major funders including American president George W. Bush's President's Emergency Plan for AIDS Relief (PEP-FAR) founded in 2003, and now the Gates Foundation. The global effort is astonishing. It has been said that there have been more than 40,000 NGOs devoted to AIDS.

Let us return to the situation at the end of the 1980s. Uganda managed to cap its epidemic, with the infection rate settling at around 7 percent. This is still staggeringly high, but well below that of southern Africa. Containment is attributed to the direct and frank way in which the matter was handled by Uganda's President Museveni, who on hearing from Fidel Castro that Ugandan soldiers sent to Cuba for training were infected, embarked on a public information campaign explaining how the disease was spread and offered strict "zero grazing" advice to men.[70] Museveni has more recently been in the news concerning possible unfair electioneering practices in Uganda, but he is credited with enlightened policy with regard to HIV infection. Equally important, however, was the civil society group TASO—the AIDS Support Organisation—founded in 1987 by

Noerine Kaleeba and colleagues, several of whom were HIV-positive, and, sadly, did not survive for long. TASO's mission is "to contribute to a process of preventing HIV infection, restoring hope and improving the quality of life of persons, families, and communities affected by HIV infection and disease," at first through counseling, support and advice, and later through the distribution of anti-retrovirals, which it now sees as a demand justified by the human right to health.[71]

The Ugandan route, tragically, was not taken in South Africa, where President Mbeki preferred to follow the arguments of Peter Duesberg, who in a wide series of writings argued that HIV could not be the cause of AIDS. Duesberg's work was at first treated with interest by at least some other scientists, and then, as more evidence became available, rejected by the scientific community. But Duesberg stuck to his guns, to the consternation of other scientists including the editor of the leading scientific journal *Nature* who personally published a rebuttal.[72] Mbeki, a believer in "African solutions for African problems," was opposed to Western medical approaches to AIDS, and especially AZT treatment, although it is less clear that he followed Duesberg in arguing that HIV was simply a "passenger virus" with no causal role in AIDS. Notoriously, as recently as 2003 Mbeki's then health minister, Tshabalala-Msimang, urged South Africans to eat beetroot, garlic, lemon, olive oil, and African potatoes to boost their immune systems rather than take anti-retroviral therapies.[73] This caused outrage and ridicule on the world stage, and dismay and embarrassment in South Africa where she became known as "Dr. Beetroot," and was trenchantly criticized by civil society groups for violating the human right to health of those who needed treatment. Offers to help from other countries were declined, leading to a health and human rights crisis.[74]

This, then, was the official climate in which the HIV/AIDS epidemic unfolded in South Africa. Unlike Uganda, where the president had given a firm lead based on long-standing principles of public health, South Africa was plunged into confusion and those diagnosed with AIDS, or fearing they had it, were susceptible to anyone offering a cure or advice. For example, the belief that sexually transmitted disease can be cured by having sex with a virgin has surfaced from time to time over the centuries.[75] Some researchers claim that this belief became widespread in South Africa, leading to child rape[76] and the rape of disabled women who were often falsely assumed to be virgins.[77] Some of the claims regarding a general belief in "virgin cleansing" have been disputed, but not the fact that the rape of young girls in South Africa was prevalent, possibly because it was thought that they presented a form of safe sex.[78] Infant rape thankfully remained very low, but the rape, or coerced or pressured sex, of young girls at the onset of sexual maturity by much older men was much more common, with a large percentage of the perpetrators schoolteachers. This brutality has resulted in a situation in which the HIV infection rate is perhaps twenty-five times higher for teenage girls than for boys.[79] It is part of a tragic spiral in which there are now millions of children in Africa living in households without adults, as AIDS has ravaged communities and left children with no surviving adult relations to look after them. Children in such situations are even more vulnerable to sexual predation by older men—not only rape but also "transactional sex," exchanging sex for food or money, and the same is true for girls who live in refugee camps.[80] Here we can see a bewildering cocktail of human rights abuses compounding each other, where the unnecessary death of parents leads to the potential destitution of children, who have to take huge and degrading risks to their health simply to survive.

In South Africa, then, the situation was ripe for an explosive rise in infections. Western countries were slow to offer help, which, in any case, the government did not seek and even rejected. As in the West it was left to civil society groups. Here the lead was taken by Treatment Action Campaign (TAC), led by the charismatic Zackie Achmat, who had previously been a successful gay rights activist, working with South Africa's first openly gay judge, Edwin Cameron. Achmat had learned a good deal from his active experience as a schoolboy in the anti-apartheid movement, and later from models of gay rights activism in the United States. He was already a seasoned campaigner when he was diagnosed as HIV-positive in 1990, and soon became embroiled in the HIV/AIDS rights movement. In 1999 he decided to go on "drug hunger strike" until ordinary South Africans could also have access to treatment.[81] The background was that the South African government's attempts to find an African solution had led to the development of a drug called Virodene, based on an industrial solvent, which was very cheap but also exceptionally toxic, never properly tested, and not approved for use. But by 1997 triple therapy was available in private clinics in South Africa, at huge cost, well beyond the means of all but the very wealthiest. Achmat saw the enormous improvement triple therapy made to the health of his friend, Judge Cameron. But watching other friends die because they could not afford the drugs that might have saved their lives led Achmat to want to take firm action. At around the same time a woman called Gugu Dlamini who had the courage to admit on radio and television that she was HIV-positive—one of the very few to speak openly about HIV/AIDs—was knifed to death by her neighbors. Achmat, with colleagues, then founded Treatment Action Campaign (TAC) with the goals of bringing medication within the reach of affordability and supporting the civil rights of people living with HIV. It was at this point that Achmat announced his own drug hunger strike.

TAC came into being in time to help support a campaign to allow South Africa to produce generic versions of essential HIV medicines without suffering trade sanctions especially from the US. The background to this was the TRIPS agreement, signed in 1994, in which all member countries of the World Trade Organization agreed to an intellectual property rights regime respecting international patent rights for twenty years. Before TRIPS, several larger developing and medium-income countries had produced generic versions of important pharmaceuticals, but continuing to do so, after an agreed transition period, would violate TRIPS. Thirty-nine pharmaceutical companies attempted to enforce their claimed patent rights against South African infringement, filing suit in 2001.[82] In response, activists accused pharmaceutical companies of violations of the human right to health by putting treatments out of financial reach, and calling on the international community to protect citizens of poor countries from these violations.

President Clinton responded to international pressure and protest in support of South Africa's policy and the suit was withdrawn. This was a major victory, and TAC and Achmat engaged in a number of ingenious stunts and protests to persuade the major companies to dramatically lower the price of HIV-related drugs, or even to donate them free of charge. But this was not enough. The government itself was the next obstacle. Mbeki's hostility to the mainstream science of HIV/AIDS meant that the drugs, though cheap or even free, would not generally be made available, for Mbeki continued to maintain that their toxicity made them too dangerous. Achmat himself was accused of being a tool of Big Pharma.[83] Or, as it was put in an extraordinary complaint laid at the International Criminal Court at The Hague in 2007 by Advocate Anthony Brink, accusing Achmat of genocide for promoting AZT and other anti-retrovirals, "Achmat directs Treatment Action Campaign ('TAC'), a professional lobby group that he founded in South Africa to shill on behalf of the multinational pharmaceutical industry by promoting the patented chemicals that it markets as so-called antiretroviral drugs ('ARVs') for the treatment of AIDS."[84]

Realizing that the ANC government, with which they had worked constructively in the past, was now blocking progress, TAC reluctantly had to consider a legal response. Here the South African situation is particularly interesting from a human rights perspective, for the right to health was included in Article 27 of the new South African constitution which took effect in 1997, and includes "the right to have access to health care services, including reproductive health care" and the right to "emergency medical treatment."[85] This is an important example where a domestic constitutional court can, in effect, hear human right to health cases. The immediate prospects, however, of a successful legal action under this head were not encouraging. The main precedent was the case of *Soobramoney v. Minister of Health*, which was brought in 1997, very soon after the adoption of the new constitution.[86] The claimant, Thiagraj Soobramoney, who was just forty-one, suffered from kidney failure and his life was in danger. He sought access to dialysis treatment at public expense in a hospital in Durban, but dialysis machines, which are very expensive, were in short supply. The hospital had set up tight guidelines for access, but he fell outside the criteria. He brought a legal action under Article 27 and in particular the right not to be denied emergency medical treatment, as well as Article 11 which states, bluntly enough, that "Everyone has the right to life."

The court emphasized, however, that even the right to life has to be understood in the context of resource constraints, and followed other precedents that it simply is not the right authority to make resource allocation decisions. Consequently the judges concentrated on the question of whether the rules applied by the hospital for access to scarce dialysis machines could be justified, and here they found no objection. The case did not succeed, and Soobramoney died just a few days after the judgment was delivered.

Given the courts' reasonable reluctance to make decisions concerning resource allocation, one might wonder whether anything is to be gained by pursuing a human right to health action. However, the position is not entirely bleak. In the Soobramoney case the judges referred to the Indian case of *Paschim Banga Khet Mazdoor Samity and others v. State of West Bengal and another*, where it was argued that the right to medical treatment falls under the constitutionally protected right to life. In this case a patient with severe head injuries was turned away from a number of state-funded hospitals and had to seek treatment at a private hospital. At least some of these state hospitals did in fact have available facilities, and denied him access on arbitrary grounds. Hence the court felt it could determine the case in the claimant's favor without distorting health resource allocation decisions.

Of course, bringing an action for the right to anti-retroviral treatment for a whole class of patients has enormous resource implications. Nevertheless, in 1999 TAC pressed for the government to make Nevirapine available to HIV-infected pregnant women in order to decrease the probability that they would pass on the infection to their child. Indeed their campaign would seem to have been supported by the constitution's Article 27(a), which provides "access to health care services, including reproductive health care." The manufacturers of Nevirapine had, in fact, offered the drug to the government free of charge for a period, so, in contrast to Soobramoney, the resource implications were very limited. The treatment is very simple: the administration of a single dose to the mother and a few drops to the baby. However, even after treatment there remains a risk of passing on infection through breastfeeding, so a comprehensive package of treatment involves replacing breastfeeding with bottle feeding, which is not a trivial matter, especially given the strong cultural attachment to breastfeeding, advocacy of breastfeeding by the World Health Organization, the cost of formula milk, and the difficulty of obtaining safe water in some parts of the country. There would also be the need for infrastructural change and staff training. Citing concerns about safety and efficacy as well as the need to assess management issues, the government allowed only small-scale pilot studies, which it was very slow to implement. The Constitutional Court accepted that there were good public health reasons for having a pilot program, but was dismayed that the infants of mothers without access to private health care were suffering while the government dragged its feet. They did not accept the government's contention that providing less than the more comprehensive package would be ineffective or harmful. Accordingly, in 2002 the court ordered the government to make Nevirapine available where it was clinically indicated to prevent transmission to infants.[87]

There are a number of important differences between Soobramoney and the TAC case. First of all, Soobramoney was an individual with a specific, fatal condition which the health service chose not to treat, even though it could have done. However, to have chosen to treat Soobramoney would have left another person facing the same plight as him, and so it was declared appropriate for the health authorities to make these decisions as long as they did so on defensible and rational grounds. In

the TAC case, the government's stand is much harder to understand. Although the government appealed to the importance
of providing a more comprehensive package of care, which
was unaffordable as well as having other difficulties, the court
was persuaded by the evidence that drug treatment, alongside
testing and counseling, would save the lives of thousands and
would have minimal cost implications. Indeed, it was argued,
there would eventually be cost savings, compared to the burden
on the health system of caring for thousands of HIV-positive
infants. It is not at all surprising that some commentators have
attempted to explain the government's position as being linked
to Mbeki's "AIDS denialism" or even the ANC's hope to be able
to provide its own, lucrative, therapy for AIDS, in the form of
the drug Virodene,[88] although such issues were not discussed in
the judgment.

Legally, then, the difference appears to be that in the Soobramoney case the authorities acted reasonably in difficult circumstances, while in the TAC case no such defense was available.
A further difference is that TAC is, after all, a campaign, building up a groundswell of support among people who themselves
were suffering from adverse government policy. TAC was able
to ride on the support of a people's movement. Human rights
cases, backed by wide, active, popular advocacy, together with
media backing, can create an unstoppable force. There was no
equivalent support for Soobramoney, even though no doubt
there was great public sympathy.

The next stage for TAC was to enter the struggle for a national
treatment plan, which also required lengthy and repeated
struggle and civil disobedience, including calling for international protests to support their campaign. A plan—far from
satisfactory—eventually came to be in late 2003, with the ambition to have 53,000 people undergoing ARV treatment within

a few months, and a program of provision of treatment centers.[89] At the same time, though, the health minister continued to express opposition to ARV treatment, looking once more to nutritional approaches. By 2005, major orders for ARV drugs were at last placed. In 2008, with Mbeki's resignation (for other reasons) as president and the appointment of a new minister of health, the plan gathered pace.

All along, TAC knew that its campaign for treatment was too narrow. Dealing with HIV/AIDS cannot be passed entirely into the hands of a health care system even if the system is strong enough to cope, which was far from the case in rural South Africa. NGO campaigns often work through elites, academics, professionals, press, and communications. TAC acted this way too, in forming alliances with trade unions and churches, but it had the essential goal of creating a situation in which "poor people become their own advocates"[90] and building a political movement for health, with an understanding of both health and governance. TAC borrowed the idea of "treatment literacy" from US AIDS activists. It requires a mass understanding of science, health, and treatment to empower ordinary people to take control of their own health. Over 200 people trained as "treatment literacy practitioners," and TAC claims to provide information for over 100,000 people per month, leading to improved understanding of how to keep oneself well, but also increasing agitation and demands for ARV treatment. Activists were typically people living with HIV, rather than professionals.[91] Hence, and by a tortuous and perilous route, South Africa is coming closer to Uganda's approach. Generally in Africa now, according to one commentator, cost is no longer the main barrier to treatment. Rather, the stigma of coming forward, together with lack of political will and weak health infrastructure, remain the most serious difficulties.[92]

It is also worth taking brief note of the situation in Botswana, South Africa's neighbor, which has a simpler story. HIV/AIDS exploded just as it did in South Africa. Indeed the proportion of people infected with HIV is even higher than in South Africa. At one time it was projected that 85 percent of fifteen-year-olds would eventually die of AIDS.[93] Yet it seems that the situation has now been significantly mitigated. Politically Botswana is an important contrast to South Africa. It peacefully gained its independence in 1966, and has been politically stable since. By GDP per capita it is one of the wealthiest countries in Africa. The impact of AIDS, however, came as a major shock, but the country did what it could to respond. By 1999–2000, AZT and Nevirapine were used to reduce mother-to-child transmission, and the effort was scaled up with help from major US universities.

Peak rates of infection in the general population in Botswana were experienced between 2000 and 2004 but since then, through a combination of government action and support from major overseas donors including the drug companies that donated their medicines, the Gates Foundation, the Merck Foundation, and the USA PEPFAR fund, HAART treatment is now generally available and the government has made huge bulk drug purchases. There are also programs to train medical staff, and programs for monitoring, evaluation, and research. Of course many questions still arise about how to implement programs and public health measures, such as whether HIV testing should be compulsory and under what circumstances, but the general picture in Botswana is of a situation over which the government has taken control.[94] Civil society action has been much less important than in South Africa, for when the government understood how it needed to act it did so, unlike the South African government, which for a long time appeared to make things worse. Indeed, just as Zackie Achmat has, absurdly, been accused of genocide for encouraging the use of anti-retroviral drugs, other commentators have more plausibly called for such charges to be laid against Thabo Mbeki for his obstructive policies, which have been said to have caused as many as 330,000 excess deaths.[95] However, the urgent task is to move forward, not to return to the past.

South Africa and Botswana are among the wealthiest countries in Africa, and have the resources to put treatment programs in place, albeit in both cases with outside assistance. It would be reasonable to doubt whether other African countries could do the same thing. Tiny and landlocked Swaziland, for example, South Africa's neighbor to the east, remains an absolute monarchy, and has nothing of the mineral wealth of many other Southern African countries. It is reported to have the world's highest rate of HIV infection, and consequently the lowest life expectancy, and, with a health system stretched desperately thin, could be expected to be virtually unable to make progress. Yet even here ways have been found to finance mass treatment campaigns, dependent, of course, on unreliable donor support, with more than half of those needing treatment now in receipt of it.[96]

Before moving on from Africa, it is worth considering issues of HIV prevention. Treating HIV infection is, of course, important, but prevention must be the ultimate goal. How is it to be achieved? The avoidance of all risky behavior would be one way, hence the emphasis on abstinence programs, led by the church and a major plank in US-funded programs until policies changed in 2008. Abstinence policies have often been criticized as hopelessly unrealistic if pursued as a sole strategy. Certainly they would need supplementation. Is education the answer? We have seen the importance of education as part of a "treatment literacy" program, and education has been used as a major element in public health strategies, yet skepticism has been expressed. For example, it has been suggested that doctors, nurses, and even AIDS counselors get infected at the same rate as the rest of the population.[97]

Condom use is clearly a very important strategy, and has further benefits in contraception and prevention of other sexually transmitted diseases. Yet it also has its limits. A wife who suspects her husband of being HIV-positive may find it very difficult to ask him to use a condom. To allow women to take more control of their vulnerability, there has been great interest in producing bactericide creams or gels. One gel, based on the drug Tenofovir, showed modest benefits in a small study in South Africa, so holds some promise, but is very far from reliable. A huge improvement in effectiveness would be needed before it could function as a major preventive strategy. But although the use of the gel is more discreet than condom use, a woman worried about being infected by her husband and using it in secret may be making herself vulnerable in other ways. For one thing, if her neighbors see that she is using it—few people in the world live with the privacy of those in American suburbs—the stigma and gossip may be destructive. And if her husband finds she has these suspicions she may well be at risk for domestic violence. Similar points could be made about a vaccine, unless it is routinely universally administered along with other childhood vaccinations. In other words, many women in the developing world are vulnerable to HIV infection precisely because they lack human rights. They are powerless to resist the sexual pressure of their husbands—a pressure enshrined even in legal norms in which husband is legal owner of wife, such as in Swaziland.[98] Accordingly, any attempt for a woman to take control of her own sexuality is fraught with danger. Here we can usefully apply one of the main ideas of General Comment

14. Medical care must be "culturally appropriate." Not only will culturally inappropriate approaches be ineffective, they may be counterproductive, even dangerous, at least until the human rights of women are strengthened in other ways.[99]

THE HIDDEN COST OF TREATING HIV/AIDS

Success in treating HIV/AIDS seems a great triumph. Despite the enormous toll the epidemic has taken, there is at least a break in the clouds. But there is another side to the story which is beginning to get increasing attention. A series of studies have pointed out that as more and more money goes to fight AIDS, as well as other diseases such as malaria and tuberculosis, in so-called "vertical programs" which focus on single conditions, there are hidden costs. For example, the number of attended births falls, as well as the number of children receiving routine inoculations. Why? The main reason is that vertical programs require staff to run them, and most of the staff need to have a previous medical training. There is always a well-founded preference for using local staff rather than flying in outsiders. But it is far from the case that in the countries we are talking about there is a surplus of trained, underutilized medical professionals looking for opportunities. Rather, every doctor or nurse recruited for a vertical program, whether by an NGO, an overseas university, or the national government, is taken away from what they were doing before.

In one of her evocative *28 Stories of AIDS in Africa*, Stephanie Nolen tells us of Tina Amisi, in the Congo:

Back then [2003], Tina Amisi was working in obstetrics and gynecology at Bukavu's public hospital—looted so many times it lacked doorknobs and mattresses and was chronically short of even the most basic medications. She leapt at the chance to work for MSF [Médecins Sans Frontières]. The salary was a draw, of course, but more than that, the clinic had all the necessary drugs and equipment. This was a chance to do real medicine, the kind she dreamed about in medical school, not the piece-meal, patchwork job she had been doing in Congo's public sys-tem. And Tina herself was a prize hire for MSF.[100]

We are used to talking and worrying about the health brain drain (which we will turn to in the next chapter), by which health workers are recruited from developing countries to wealthy ones, but the silent internal brain drain may be equally damag-ing. For this reason there is now a turn within the human right to health movement toward the idea of "health system strength-ening" or "horizontal programs" rather than vertical programs. Inevitably this will mean fewer people will be treated, or treated as quickly, for HIV/AIDS. Understanding these issues may make one despair of acting for the better. But if the problems were easy, we would have solved them long ago.

CONCLUSION

As we saw in earlier chapters, it is now part of the usual analysis of human rights to see them as generating three types of duties: duties to respect, to protect, and to fulfill. By way of concluding this chapter it will be helpful to apply this analysis to the story of HIV/AIDS and human rights.

The duty to respect requires the government not to act in ways that interfere directly with the enjoyment of the right. In other contexts, for example, a government fails to respect the rights of a citizen if it bans their religion. Failure to respect the right to health is rarely so clear-cut, except in cases of tyrannical governments victimizing unpopular minorities. It is unusual for a democratically elected government deliberately to take steps that will impair the health of its citizens (as distinct from failing to take steps to improve their health), although arguably the banning of abortion or, in the case of HIV/AIDS, condoms could fall into this category. The South African government came close to failing to respect the right to health of its citizens in its initial promotion of the untested and highly toxic drug Virodene, although its delay in offering ARV drugs is a failure to fulfill rather than to respect.

In many other cases, the failure to respect rights in relation to HIV/AIDS has been a matter of failing to respect other human rights, such as freedom of movement and reproductive freedom. We have looked at various attempts to restrict the activities of people diagnosed with, or suspected of, infection. These include such things as refusal to admit people living with HIV into the country and criminalizing their sexual behavior. This goes as far as forced sterilization of women living with HIV, of which, in Namibia for example, there are recent documented cases.[101]

There is, though, a double complication. First, restricting the activities of people with HIV was not discrimination pure and simple; it was attempted in order to protect the rights to health of the great majority of the population who were not infected. We cannot take it for granted that doing this is always wrong. Had HIV been transmissible in the way in which, say, the flu virus is, then much greater restrictions on activity would surely have been justified. As it turned out, most of the restrictions were panic measures with no scientific basis, but it might have been otherwise. Second, as Jonathan Mann argued from early on, restrictive measures are likely to be counterproductive. If people diagnosed as HIV-positive lose their houses or jobs, who is going to come forward for testing? This drives the disease underground, where it is an even greater public health problem. In the end there is no justification for discriminatory measures against people living with HIV, but this was a lesson many governments found very hard to learn. The first threat, then, to people with HIV is unjustified discrimination by their own governments.

The second duty falling on governments is the duty to protect. Part of this is a matter of protecting citizens from the violation of their right to health by others. Here, for example, governments may have a duty to enforce regulations on insurance companies to prevent them from denying insurance renewal to those with HIV/AIDS, as we saw in the case of the USA. It also includes protecting people living with HIV from the often vicious prejudice of those around them, especially if this would be detrimental to health. This can include neighbors, as we saw in the case of teenager Ryan White, or extended family members as has often been the case in Africa.[102] Here it can be very hard for governments to act. It may be possible for governments to regulate commercial organizations such as insurance companies, and to strengthen employment and housing protection as the US has done. But changing attitudes and policing private behavior is a much more difficult matter. Still, progress is possible, through education, role models, and examples (such as images of Princess Diana shaking hands with an AIDS patient in 1987). The complexity of the task means it is a long process, but this is not a reason for giving up.

A second aspect of the right to protect is the duty to prevent onward infection. As we have just seen, governments have often interpreted this as providing justification for restrictions on the behavior of people in risk groups. Generally, it will mean putting in place public health measures—education, easy accessibility of condoms—that will help reduce infection. Once more matters are not entirely straightforward, in that apparently sensible policies can have negative effects. Abstinence campaigns may lead to secretive, unprotected sex. Male circumcision which reduces the risk of female-to-male transmission can encourage risky behavior. The difficulty with trying to influence people's behavior is that in many cases people are as weak as their weakest moment, when temptation overrides education.[103]

The duty to fulfill includes the supply of treatment that is safe and effective. Wealthy countries have, for the most part, worked out how to do this. The story for the developing world is highly instructive in understanding how human rights duties develop. In the first instance, the duty to provide treatment falls on the national government. But many governments cannot afford to pay for treatment. One possible response is to appeal to the idea of "progressive realization," in which lack of resources provides a cast-iron excuse. Although these arguments were made, in practice most countries saw things differently. Saving the lives of their citizens was viewed more as a human rights core obligation, and resource constraint was no excuse for failure. Accordingly, two lines of action were tried in combination. First, various attempts were made to bring down the price of expensive medications. Second, appeal was made to the international community to help.

We see here the pattern of action described earlier. Recall that one area of skepticism about human rights is the question of who has the corresponding duties. Our answer was that in the first instance it always falls on the national government. Only if the national government fails to do what it should does it spread further. If the government is unwilling to meet its duty—as in the case of South Africa—then the international community has a duty to apply pressure to bring it to act as it should. If the government is willing but unable, as in other African countries, then the international community has a duty to assist. At last, we see that it is doing so, as in the case of Botswana, where we noted that drug companies agreed to lower their prices and external funders put up some of the money toward the treatment program.

The duty to fulfill the human right to health also gives governments a duty to put structures in place to make it possible to advance health on something like a routine basis. Laws that provide rights to treatment, and the provision and staffing of clinics that make high quality treatments available, are called for. Developed nations managed to do this, albeit at different speeds, but for many developing nations the challenge is still ahead. Uganda took some early, far from complete, steps in this direction, and Botswana has probably gone the furthest in Africa. Complete fulfillment of the right to health turns an urgent political and social issue into a routine government and medical matter.

HIV/AIDS and the human right to health, we noted at the start of this chapter, emerged and developed together. Before the AIDS epidemic the human right to health was barely understood, either as a philosophical concept or as a focus for activism. The profound health emergency of AIDS, and the fact that it hit, at first, a stigmatized but articulate and radicalized segment of the population, brought forth new organizations with a need to develop tools to lobby and pressure governments to act. The idea of human rights was ready to hand, but was used first only in claims for protection against discrimination toward people living with HIV. But this, as we saw, had public health benefits. Removing stigma also reduces the barriers against people coming forward for testing, and those who knew that they were HIV-positive were more likely to change their behavior. Once treatments became available, this first wave of human rights activism was supplemented by a vital second wave, in the form of advocacy for the human right to access to treatment, and for people living with HIV to have much more control over their own health and treatment. The path developed by early HIV/AIDS activists became a model for human right to health campaigns throughout the globe in relation to many different health threats, as we will explore in the next chapter.

If in the developed world, rights against discrimination were claimed and broadly respected even before the right to treatment had any focus, in the developing world there is a case that the right to treatment is actually more advanced than rights against discrimination. Anti-retroviral drugs are increasingly available, yet a very high proportion of Africans living with HIV have not come forward for testing; most of the cited figures for prevalence are estimates. Until discrimination against people known to be living with HIV is removed, infection rates will continue to be high. Furthermore, other human rights abuses, such as sexual violence against women, intensify the problem. Finding the money to pay for treatment can be less difficult than getting people to admit that they need treatment in the first place, and it may be harder still to keep dependent and powerless people safe from infection. Ironically, then, what was in the developed world the final human rights victory—access to treatment—is closer to achievement in Africa than the struggle for civil and political rights for people living with HIV and those highly vulnerable to infection.

Chapter 4

PROBLEMS AND PROSPECTS

I f, in the early 1980s, campaigning in terms of the human right to health would have been unthinkable, the landscape now has changed dramatically. Just to take the academic literature, a new journal called *Health and Human Rights* was founded in 1994, first edited by Jonathan Mann and now by Paul Farmer, and is available online and open-access. Established and highly respected journals such as *The Lancet*, *The British Medical Journal* and *The New England Journal of Medicine* regularly publish articles promoting the human right to health. Recent articles have highlighted human right to health issues in, to name just a few, Burma, Gaza, Ecuador, Cambodia, Mexico, Argentina, the Netherlands, the USA, and Nepal. Groups suffering particular problems include women, children, asylum seekers, prisoners, gypsies, disabled people, indigenous groups, deaf people, lesbians and drug addicts. Alleged violators include not only governments but Big Pharma, donors, international financial institutions, the medical profession, medical educators, and private companies. And specific concerns have been raised about malaria, neglected tropical diseases, essential surgery, polio and compulsory vaccination, substance abuse, maternal mortality, and female general mutilation, again just to name some of the more prominent examples.

Over the decades activists have made a number of charges that could hardly be more important: people are dying unnecessarily in their millions. The world has not stood still. In some of the highest-profile issues, the critics have won the argument. A familiar pattern of complaint and response has emerged. First, an issue is highlighted by activists, whether NGOs, concerned medical staff, or even governments themselves. Against official fatalism that little, if anything, can be done, small-scale initiatives provide a model for what might be possible. International institutions and donors wake up and sponsor research. Position papers are issued, voluntary codes sought, and by some means or other the world community begins to find ways of taking its responsibilities seriously. In most cases, very sadly, we are not yet at a stage where we can show that the burden of disease has been dramatically reduced, but there are many promising signs. Often, of course, action has turned out to be ineffective, inappropriate, or even counterproductive, and sometimes a matter of mitigating damage rather than making new progress. But all of this is progress of a sort. In the remainder of this chapter we will look at some of the most widely discussed case studies and draw conclusions that can help guide our thinking where new issues emerge.

THE WORLD BANK AND HEALTH SYSTEMS

The World Bank, alongside the International Monetary Fund (IMF), was set up as a result of the Bretton Woods Conference in 1944, as part of a program to finance the rebuilding of Europe after the Second World War. This is not the place to enter into a general discussion of World Bank policies or, as former World Bank economist Joseph Stiglitz argues, whether the real villain is the IMF,[1] but it is the place to explore how World Bank policies affected health, and in particular the ability of developing countries to meet their duties to protect and fulfill the right to health of their citizens.

In the 1950s and 1960s, large infrastructure projects were the bank's preferred development strategy, but in the 1970s, under the leadership of Robert McNamara, health became more prominent in its activities. In 1974 it sponsored a successful project, which turned out to last for thirty years, to eliminate river blindness in West Africa. The bank's World Development Report of 1980 emphasized the importance of health and the ability of governments to tackle problems if given sufficient assistance. In 1993, in a major development, health became the main focus of the World Development Report, which that year was entitled *Investing in Health*. By 2004 it could be written that "the World Bank is now the world's largest external funder of health, committing more than $1 billion annually in new lending to improve health, nutrition, and population in developing countries. Moreover, it is one of the world's largest external funders of the fight against HIV/AIDS, with current commitments of more than $1.3 billion, 50 percent of that to sub-Saharan Africa."[2]

The World Bank must be given credit for taking bold and

imaginative steps that have reduced the global burden of disease. Yet critics point out that underneath this triumphalism is a darker side. In the mid-1980s, in the era of the governments of Ronald Reagan in the USA and Margaret Thatcher in the UK, the World Bank and the IMF became gripped by what is often called "market fundamentalism" or "the Washington Consensus." This is represented by its critics as a "one-size-fits-all" approach to development in which macroeconomic stability, free markets, trade liberalization, and shrinking the public sector are seen as the route to economic growth and the end of poverty. The programs, now so reviled in the development movement, are known as "structural adjustment,"[3] and are intended to bring a type of economic stability to a country, controlling inflation and making it more attractive to external investors.

Whatever sound theory there may have been behind the practice, and whatever good structural adjustment might have done in other respects, it is widely argued that structural adjustment has been a disaster for health, at least in some of the poorest countries of the world.[4] At best, one might see the World Bank's policies as a tragic misapplication of the ideas of the social determinants of health.[5] Once it is noted that, for poor countries, there is an impressive correlation between wealth, as measured by GDP per capita, and health indicators, it may appear that the best way to achieve good health outcomes is to do whatever is necessary to drive growth. This was, however, doubly problematic and seems to have turned out to be a gross and fatal oversimplification.

First, the World Bank often required countries to reduce public spending, including spending on health, as part of the structural adjustment to drive economic growth. Whatever the long-term effects, the shorter-term consequences on health are unlikely to be encouraging. Reduction in public spending on health is often accompanied by charging user fees to the patient. Basic economics should reveal that any price may be too high for some people, and if they don't have access to the money they cannot buy the service, even if they are in severe need. User fees quite obviously lead to lower take-up of services.[6] Pressing the criticism in detail, an analysis of World Bank policies written in 2004 notes that according to the World Bank's own figures, a health budget of US$13 per person per year was needed for a country to meet its core obligations related to health. The authors then point out that "In Mozambique, per capita health expenditure fell from US$3.50 in 1986 to US$0.68 in 1988—after the introduction of a structural adjustment program in 1987. . . . one can only conclude that SAPs resulted in retrogression in realizing the right to health in many developing nations."[7] Indeed, UNICEF estimated that structural adjustment had led to 500,000 child deaths in twelve months, although the World Bank's own research, not surprisingly, questions the evidence.[8]

I mentioned a double flaw in the World Bank's argument that cutting health services to advance economic growth would be beneficial to health. The first was the damage done by cutting health services. The second is that structural adjustment has not, in general, been successful in eliminating poverty. It is often claimed that the World Bank and the IMF have made no significant inroads on poverty. More accurately, growth in GDP per capita has often been achieved, but the distribution of wealth in many countries can be so unequal that poverty for the masses remains unchanged. Short-term pain has not generated the hoped-for long-term gain.

To see how structural adjustment works in more detail, consider the World Bank report *Investing in Health*, published in 1993. It sets out a three-pronged program for improving health.

The first sounds broadly admirable, even though it is worded in a way that triggers alarm bells:

> First, governments need to foster an economic environment that enables households to improve their own health. Growth policies (including, where necessary, economic adjustment policies) that ensure income gains for the poor are essential. So, too, is expanded investment in schooling, particularly for girls.[9]

The second element is a recommendation for governments to reassign spending from high-tech hospital-based services to much more cost-effective public health initiatives. Many welcomed this approach, but nevertheless critics were worried about the notion of cost-effectiveness applied to health. The danger, of course, is that on cost-effectiveness grounds people in low-resource environments might be deemed not cost-effective to treat, if health budgets are low and the cost of treating them is high.[10] But the third element, so critics allege, spoils whatever promise there is in the first two, and must be quoted at length:

> Third, governments need to promote greater diversity and competition in the financing and delivery of health services. Government financing of public health and essential clinical services would leave the coverage of remaining clinical services to private finance, usually mediated through insurance, or to social insurance. Government regulation can strengthen private insurance markets by improving incentives for wide coverage and for cost control. Even for publicly financed clinical services, governments can encourage competition and private sector involvement in service supply and can help improve the efficiency of the private sector by generating and disseminating key information. The combination of these measures will improve

health outcomes and contain costs while enhancing consumer satisfaction.[11]

It is not hard to believe that many national health systems are complacent and inefficient, and where there is a large or dispersed population may have great difficulty providing anything like universal coverage of many health services. Mainstream economic theory would predict that opening up the health sector to competition from the private sector could have beneficial effects. But even if this is true for some countries, in others, the poorest, and where the burden of disease is highest, it simply seems beside the point. It is hard to believe that the main problem with health services in the world's poorest countries is lack of competition in the health sector, leading to diminished "consumer satisfaction." Who could believe that children are dying in Liberia and Angola because of the lack of diversity and competition in financing and delivery of health services? What evidence is there that privatizing health care leads to improved health outcomes or cost containment, never mind both together? The self-confidence with which these claims are asserted is staggering. The failure of such policies was not a surprise. And it is not surprising that critics saw a double meaning in the title *Investing in Health*: not only an assertion that the people's health is an investment, but also an invitation to private business to find ways of profiting from health policy in the developing world.[12]

In the interest of balance we should note that structural adjustment programs were often introduced at times of severe financial crisis, making it hard to know whether they really did do as much harm as claimed. What we need to understand is not how things were before, but rather, how they would have been if some alternative program was followed—and this is something we can never really know. In any case, the critics won the argument and structural adjustment ended in the mid-1990s. Have lessons been learned since? The World Bank's program after 1999 allowed developing countries more "ownership" of their economic plans, yet according to critics continued to make it very difficult for countries to raise enough money to meet their core human rights obligations. Countries that could not afford to meet the minimum standard looked to overseas aid for help, but the World Bank was worried—perhaps rightly—that large-scale foreign aid would cause macroeconomic problems. Experience elsewhere suggests that large influxes of foreign currency ruin export industries, and so, as export is a main hope for future development, extensive financial aid can be self-defeating in the long run.[13] Therefore, the World Bank continued to cap government health expenditure.[14] If this theory is right, then there is a serious dilemma. Should a country seek longer-term economic growth, even if this means neglecting current health needs? Or should present urgent needs have priority, especially as economic prophecy is so uncertain? Perhaps more importantly, should it be the role of the World Bank to pressurise a country into making the decision one way rather than the other? Some critics make the provocative claim that not only does the World Bank violate the human right to health by putting macroeconomic factors before the right to health, but that donor countries to the World Bank have been equally culpable.[15] Furthermore, the World Bank has been accused of allowing "leakage" of funds from the health sector on a huge scale, so that in many sub-Saharan African countries, money designated for health expenditure simply never reaches its destination, and the World Bank has done little to investigate or take steps to remedy the situation.[16] Even the World Bank's own internal evaluation admits, "The accountability of Bank and

IFC-financed HNP [Health, Nutrition and Poverty] projects to ensure that results actually reach the poor has been weak."[17] The evaluation report goes on to suggest that a significant number of projects that were justified in the name of poverty reduction in fact had no internal mechanism to identify and target the poor, and so the benefits tended to go to people who were not regarded as poor. For example, a sanitation project in Nepal was intended to improve the health of the poor, but in reality the project only assisted communities that lived alongside main roads, whereas the poorest people tended to live in more remote areas.[18]

For decades the World Bank and the International Monetary Fund have been accused of doing harm to the health of the poor by preventing their governments from pursuing beneficial health policies. Due to concerted criticism the period of the greatest damage is over. But the jury is still out on the question of whether, in the area of health, the World Bank and the IMF have yet shown significant results for their efforts. Still, it does appear that its critics have forced a retreat from the most damaging policies, and the World Bank and the IMF's willingness to listen to criticism, and to engage in self-criticism, is encouraging.

TRIPS AND THE PRICE OF MEDICINES

Human right to health activists often pay a great deal of attention to the underlying determinants of health and illness, such as poverty and illiteracy. Yet once people have become ill, a cure is needed. The WHO maintains a list of essential medicines that should be available in all countries. Millions of people die through lack of access to such medicines, even though most of the medicines on the list are not at all costly for governments and are off-patent so available in generic form. Lack of access to medicine is often, then, a problem of organization and infrastructure, not a problem of cost. Nevertheless, in a significant number of cases cost is a major problem—and it is more of a problem than it was two decades ago.

Prior to the 1990s, many developing countries did not recognize patents or copyrights that had been granted in other countries. In India, Brazil, and other large developing countries with industrial capability, it was standard practice to develop generic versions of pharmaceuticals that would otherwise have been available only at an unaffordable price. However, the World Trade Organization, the third Bretton Woods institution and the last to play a major role on the world stage, has attempted to bring in a level of harmonization of intellectual property. The main instrument by which this has been done is known as TRIPS—Trade Related Aspects of Intellectual Property Rights. (One might think that a more appropriate shortening of the name would have been TRAPS, but this would have given the game away.) TRIPS was negotiated in 1994. Membership of the WTO is seen as advantageous in gaining access to world markets, and TRIPS is binding on all members. The essence of TRIPS is that although there are various transitional exemptions, mostly expired now, the aim is to move to a world in which all countries respect international copyrights and patents. The agreement included a twenty-year patent period for new medicines, allowing the producer company a temporary monopoly during which it can set its own price without having to worry about competition. Countries cannot pick and choose which provisions to follow, and so while it may be beneficial to trade to be a member of the WTO, it provides a great challenge to countries that simply do not have the resources to purchase novel medicines at full price; they will be unable to meet their obligation to fulfill the right to health for their citizens. Arguably, then, all signatories of TRIPS have failed to protect the human right to health by allowing drug companies to charge unaffordable prices for essential medicines. Although TRIPS does allow for "compulsory licensing" of patented medicines in cases of national emergency, in practice this provision is rarely used.[19] However, Brazil has managed to make low-cost, generic HIV treatments available, and a complaint against Brazil in 2001 from the USA to the WTO was withdrawn,[20] most likely because of the likely world outrage if the USA had managed to make HIV treatment unaffordable in Brazil, leading to the early deaths of tens of thousands.

Although Big Pharma is portrayed as the villain of this story it is important to understand why drug companies feel they need this period of patent. While manufacturing a drug may not be enormously expensive, the cost of research and development can be phenomenal. And it must be recognized that most research undertaken by pharmaceutical companies never issues in a commercial product. Hence the loss they make on other lines of research must be recouped from the very few successful products. If they were not permitted a temporary monopoly position they simply could not afford to research, and the supply of new medicines would dry up completely. The real dilemma, then, is how to allow access without destroying the industry.

To explore this further it is worth looking at the example of drug-resistant tuberculosis. Tuberculosis has been known since ancient times, and is one of a host of infectious diseases that blighted our ancestors. According to medical historian Roy Porter, "until the nineteenth century, towns were so insanitary that their populations never replaced themselves by reproduction, multiplying themselves only thanks to the influx of rural surpluses who were tragically infection-prone."[21] Tuberculosis may have been one of the main killers: in Paris hospitals at the beginning of the nineteenth century it was said to be the cause of 40 percent of deaths.[22] Although public health measures, such as campaigns to end spitting in public places and the opening of sanatoria, were attempted in the latter part of the century, death rates remained high. But in the first half of the twentieth century a whole raft of public health measures, from the provision of clean water to the placing of lids on dustbins, created a much more hygienic urban atmosphere and TB infection rates plummeted.[23] The discovery of antibiotics used in combination finally provided an effective means of treating TB.[24] Further refinements have led to more successful attempts to cure TB and reduce the chance of resistant strains forming.

In one sense, then, TB is a great success story of medical science. Yet today around 1.5 million people a year die of TB. Why is that? Not all cases will respond to medication and, of course, many people in the developing world do not receive treatment. Furthermore, drug-resistant strains of TB are on the rise and now cause about 10 percent of these deaths.

The possibility that patients could develop resistance to antibiotics was a problem from the start, which is why the antibiotics were used in combination. As early as 1958, it was known that drug-resistant TB could result from poor prescription practices and poor adherence to treatment protocols and could, therefore, lead to resistant strains emerging in the general population.[25] The warning, though, was not enough, and the feared outcome of careless practices has been realized. Drug-resistant tuberculosis, we already noted, is killing about 150,000 people a year. These conditions can be traced back to several decades of poor use of antibiotics: disease induced through medical means. And susceptibility to TB in all its forms is compounded with the HIV/AIDS epidemic.

To improve adherence to therapy, "DOTS"—directly observed treatment short-course—has been developed, in which a "treatment partner" watches and makes a record of the patient taking their medication. Yet many patients have what is known as multi-drug-resistant tuberculosis (MDRTB) which is resistant to at least two of the normal first-line drugs. This condition is now widespread and often affects people who have previously been treated for TB, indicating either that they were given the wrong initial diagnosis or that their treatment caused the development of a new resistant strain. Paul Farmer, for example, reports on something close to an epidemic ravaging Russian prisons in the 1990s. He notes that patients likely to have MDRTB were nevertheless being treated with standard first line therapies, which would be not only ineffective but likely to encourage even more resistant strains to emerge. Add to this the hugely overcrowded conditions in Russian prisons and there is a perfect breeding ground for infection.

First-line therapy for TB is relatively cheap and often effective. Second-line therapy is much more problematic. It can cost up to one hundred times as much, perhaps tens of thousands of dollars per person, and takes much longer to deliver results as well as being more toxic to the patient. Nevertheless, Paul Farmer, with the group Partners in Health, had shown in 1992 in Peru that it was possible to use second-line therapy to treat cases that previously were thought to be untreatable.[26] He had managed to find donors to pay for treatment for a small group, just fifty patients, with excellent results, and was ready to scale up treatment. But in "low-resource settings," such as Russian prisons, much of this treatment was deemed unaffordable or not cost-effective and so patients were simply left to die.

Cost-effectiveness is the bugbear of every health system. No health system can offer every possible therapy, even when theoretically it is available. But, Paul Farmer asks, why are these treatments not cost-effective? Why are they so expensive? And why is there no money? In the case of Russian prisoners, Farmer points out that the drugs are expensive because of the decisions of drug companies, and Russia has little money available partly as a result of the dismantling of its health system under the orders of the World Bank and partly because of the redistribution of wealth with huge amounts of cash in the hands of its elite flowing out of Russia to New York, Switzerland, and the Caribbean. These are not natural facts but the result of human decisions: decisions that lead to the neglect—violation—of the human right to health.[27]

We have already reviewed some of the issues connected with the World Bank. Let us instead consider how the world might have responded before TRIPS. Quite possibly a pharmaceutical company in, say, India would have obtained samples of the new drugs, and devised ways of producing generic versions. These could then have been made available throughout the developing world to the great benefit of huge numbers of people. The TRIPS agreement, it seems, makes such an approach highly problematic for any drug under patent, although the later Doha Declaration and some other modifications do provide some exceptions in case of epidemics.[28] (We should note, however, that Russia is not bound by TRIPS as it is not a member of the WTO, but TRIPS has made generic versions of patented drugs less generally available.)

Some people have argued that the current situation is so

problematic that we need an entirely new approach to international patents. Philosopher Thomas Pogge, for example, has put forward a proposal for a highly ingenious Health Impact Fund, in which pharmaceutical companies can opt for a different type of patent arrangement. In this approach, companies would receive payment not only for their drugs but also for the good they do: their "health impact." Accordingly, drug companies would bring down prices to maximize distribution and also, perhaps, encourage licensed generic production and research for neglected diseases where there is the most good still to be done.[29] However, moving to a new international patent system would be a hugely complex task, and it is not entirely clear how this new approach would be funded. Pogge accepts that it would be highly expensive, but looks to wealthy countries to fund it as part of their human rights obligations. Unfortunately, whether funds would be forthcoming on a sufficient scale in any sustained fashion is highly uncertain.

In practice a different, dual strategy has been adopted: price differentiation and direct support from donors. Price differentiation is a matter of charging different prices for the same good. This is well known as a commercial strategy. Theatres will often sell seats to students on the day at a discount: it is better to raise some revenue than to have empty seats. Equally a drug company may feel that it is better to sell a drug at a lower price in a poor country than to charge a high price but to make very few sales. They might even be prepared to sell at cost price, as part of a "corporate social responsibility" program, and for the goodwill that will accrue. But there is, of course, a huge commercial danger. Drugs bought in one market can be moved to another, and hence a black market in cheap drugs may appear elsewhere. If this were to happen it would be to give up the advantages of the patent system. Hence, if price differentiation is to be employed, it needs to be done so in a highly controlled and regulated fashion.

Indeed, this is what we are starting to see. Aware of the dangers, drug companies typically do not allow low-price drugs on to the open market. Rather they work with institutions, NGOs and donors such as the World Health Organization or Médicins Sans Frontières to bring low-price drugs to target groups. Multi-drug-resistant TB turns out to be an excellent example of this strategy. The World Health Organization has declared that treating MDRTB, and indeed the even more serious XDRTB (extensively drug-resistant TB) is cost-effective.[30] Funding has been made available through the Global Fund for HIV, Malaria, and Tuberculosis, and drug companies have provided medicines at lower prices through a pathway set up by the WHO and MSF called the Green Light Committee Initiative, which started in 2000. Although the amount flowing so far is nowhere near enough to offer everyone treatment, it is a major move in overcoming the high price of drugs without destabilizing the commercial market. Related projects include an internationally funded initiative to ensure that all countries have the laboratory facilities to diagnose different forms of TB. Current targets are for 80 percent of all drug-resistant cases to be treated by 2015.[31] This is optimistic and, perhaps, highly unlikely to be met, but it is a powerful indication that human rights campaigns, accompanied by civil society initiatives showing what can be achieved, can stir international organizations into action. Governments can be urged, pushed and helped into meeting their obligations to protect and fulfill the human right to health. Similar initiatives are being attempted with malaria funding, for example.[32]

In fact, drug companies donating their products on a significant scale is nothing new. Even in 2002, the Nuffield Council on Bioethics could give examples of donations of therapies for river blindness, elephantiasis, trachoma, and malaria, as well as contraceptives and condoms.[33] What is new is the scale of funds now available from donors and multinational organizations to spread the financial cost.

THE HEALTH BRAIN DRAIN

In the World Health Report for 2006, the WHO calculated that there was a world shortfall of 2.4 million doctors, nurses, and midwives, and 4.3 million health workers in total, with much of sub-Saharan Africa in deepest crisis.[34] Many smaller African countries do not have their own medical schools to train doctors and so must rely on attracting doctors trained elsewhere.[35]

The shortage of health workers is bad enough in its own right. It has been argued that it compromises the quality of health care in other ways:

> The economies of most developing countries cannot sustain adequate medical staffs to meet the demand for health services. The few medical staff who can be retained are so valuable that the system cannot conceive of disciplining them for substandard practices. In many cases, qualified, dedicated medical professionals are frustrated by long hours of work for meager salaries. Patients are too scared to make any noise, lest they cut themselves off from the opportunity for medical care in the future. To the extent that resources remain this limited in our developing countries, it will be extremely difficult to achieve health and human rights for all.[36]

What is the global community doing to help the developing world make it good its failure to fulfill the right to health of so many of its citizens? Although efforts have been made to increase the numbers of people in the developing world receiving a medical education, broadly over the last couple of decades the wealthiest countries have been making matters worse through the international recruitment of health workers. Predicting a chronic shortage in the supply of future health workers, countries of the developed world undertook active overseas recruitment drives. Part of the shortage in nurses in the developed world stemmed from the expansion of other opportunities for women in the labor market, which made nursing a much less obvious career choice than it had been in the past. At the same time several developed countries were greatly increasing their investment in health, in the face of an aging population and a rise in chronic disease. To deal with the perceived lack of doctors and nurses they looked abroad. For example, a report by the UK King's Fund in 2004 states that "In 2002 nearly half of the 10,000 new full registrants on the General Medical Council (GMC) register [i.e. doctors] were from abroad; in 2003 this had risen to more than two-thirds of 15,000 registrants. Most of the growth has been in doctors from non-European Economic Area countries."[37]

The situation elsewhere is similar. For decades about 25 percent of doctors practicing in the USA received their training elsewhere. This now amounts to close to 200,000 doctors educated outside the USA. Around 5,000 were trained in sub-Saharan Africa, predominately, but not exclusively, Ghana, Nigeria and South Africa. In 2002 there were forty-seven Liberian-trained doctors working in the US, and just seventy-two working in Liberia.[38] A parallel, though less dramatic, story can be told for nursing staff. In Canada, New Zealand, and Australia the picture is the same. In fact, there are patterns of chains of migration: the USA recruits from Canada, Canada from South Africa, and South Africa from the rest of Africa.[39] Ultimately the shortage will be felt by the poorest. The WHO lists ten countries that lose more than 50 percent of their trained doctors, including Haiti, Sierra Leone, Angola, and Mozambique.[40]

In most countries, especially in the developing world, doctors are trained at public expense. If a doctor from Ghana is recruited to the USA, not only does Ghana lose its doctor, it loses the money paid for the training. Now it may be that the doctor is likely to send a portion of earnings back home (known in the development business as remittances). But this is scant compensation. Not only is the developed world reducing the ability of countries in the developing world to meet their duty to fulfill the right to health, they are taking a massive hidden financial subsidy from them. Furthermore, the emigration of skilled professionals is problematic from the point of view of civil society and democracy; doctors and nurses are respected and influential members of their societies. They are intelligent people and often have a sense of civic responsibility (which partially explains their career choice). They are a force for stability, but also for beneficial reform in their own countries. However much money they send back home, and even if health clinics are staffed by Western volunteers, nothing can make up for their loss.[41]

What can be done? Recognition of the problem is the first step. In some circles it has been known for many years, but in the last decade or so acknowledgment has widened and deepened. Complaints from Africa have, at the minimum, made the developed world uncomfortable enough to want at least to be seen to be doing something. One relatively early response was a code of practice adopted in 2003 by the ministers of health of all the fifty or so member states of the Commonwealth, which includes the UK, Australia, Canada, New Zealand,

South Africa, Nigeria, Uganda, India, Pakistan, Bangladesh, and many other African, Caribbean, Asian, and South Pacific states. This is the residue of the British Empire: predominantly English-speaking countries with similar education systems and a practice of permitting immigration, and so historically a great source of migrant labor. The Commonwealth Code of Practice recognizes the individual and social benefits of a mobile labor force, not only in terms of individual ambition but also in the return of staff who have learned new skills abroad. Hence it does not restrict rights of individuals to move. However it encourages governments to agree to an ethical framework which provides benefits to both sides. It appears that the UK has taken this approach seriously. The NHS applied these ideas beyond the Commonwealth and adopted the policy of recruiting nurses only from countries that signed agreements and considered themselves to have a surplus of trained staff. Such agreements were signed with Spain, some countries in Eastern Europe, and the Philippines, which has a deliberate policy of training a surplus of nurses. Accordingly, recruitment of nurses from South Africa fell from 2,114 in 2002 to thirty-nine in 2007.[42] It has to be noted, though, that like any system it has loopholes. The relatively small private sector in the UK is not bound by these agreements and still recruits from the global market. Once medical staff are present in the UK, it is easier for them to switch into the National Health Service.

Still, substantial progress has been made, and at the same time the UK declared that it would help train more medical staff in the developing world and made it easier for British health workers to spend time abroad. Perhaps most importantly of all, it decided to increase the number of medical students trained in the UK by opening new medical schools, thereby reducing the "pull factor": the need actively to recruit. Some have criticized the UK for doing this, for there was a period where there appeared to be a huge oversupply of doctors. However, changes to the visa system seem to have allowed matters to settle down and the UK has no need actively to recruit overseas-trained doctors. With a few exceptions—Norway has been cited in this regard—other developed countries have responded more slowly, and so this is still a work in progress.[43] Nevertheless, the World Health Authority has passed a number of similar resolutions starting in 2004, progressing through the World Health Report in 2006, and culminating in 2010, with a Global Code of Practice.[44] Like the Commonwealth Code it is a voluntary code, and so can be ignored without sanction. But it is a recognition that something is stirring in this area.

Country-to-country migration is not the only problem of the brain drain. All countries struggle with the fact that on the whole doctors would rather live in cities than in rural locations, and, within cities, in wealthier parts of town. This was identified many years ago by British doctor Julian Tudor Hart as the "inverse care law": those who are in the least medical need have the greatest access to doctors. It is a simple consequence of freedom of choice for medical staff, and can be overcome only by compulsion, persuasion, or financial incentives. All of these have been tried with varying degrees of success.

Much more important, though, is the issue discussed in the last chapter: the effect of vertical programs on health systems. When a new, well-funded program opens in a country it needs trained staff, and it will take them away from their current work. Health workers, like anyone else, will respond to incentives of higher money, but perhaps even more important for them is the opportunity to work in a well-equipped environment. The consequence, of course, is that the residue of the health system loses its best people, causing further decline.

These difficulties have been identified and publicized widely only in the last few years, but they have bubbled up to the attention of the World Health Organization.[45] Since the 1960s it has been known that vertical programs will be relatively unsuccessful in the longer term unless followed up with a more general strengthening of the health care system.[46] The complaint now is not simply about long-term ineffectiveness, but the long- and short-term damage of attracting staff to externally funded programs. The WHO itself points to examples:

> In Ethiopia, contract staff hired to help implement programmes were paid three times more than regular government employees, while in Malawi, a hospital saw 88 nurses leave for better paid nongovernmental organization (NGO) programmes in an 18-month period.[47]

Inevitably recruitment of health workers to vertical programs will lead to a degradation in routine care.

Yet, once again, the picture is mixed. The WHO claims there are examples where vertical programs have been harmonized with local priorities to strengthen health systems.[48] The first step, as always, is to be aware of the damage that may be done as an unintended consequence of good intentions, and wherever possible to guard against it.

It is also said that international organizations such as the WHO are creating problems. Some of the most experienced and influential doctors from developing countries are appointed to high-level posts in Geneva, where they sit at a desk writing reports and making recommendations rather than attending directly to the health needs of their compatriots. Whether this is a fair criticism is not so clear. There is often a tendency to denigrate anything except "front-line care," but in fact we have seen that much of the global burden of disease is a failure of policy, infrastructure, and organization. There are cases where good management can do much more good than good health care. And bad management can do very much more harm than bad health care.

In summary, for a number of reasons health systems in the developing world have become weakened by a chronic shortage of health workers, and this has been exacerbated by external and internal brain drains. These undermine a country's ability to fulfill its right to health duties, and, rather than aiding them to fill the gap, wealthy countries have been making things worse. There are some promising attempts to stop the flow and repair health systems, but a great deal remains to be done.

RESEARCH ETHICS

A famous claim from the 1990s was that there was a 10/90 gap in research funding for health: that is, less than 10 percent of research funding was devoted to the conditions that afflicted low- and middle-income countries where 90 percent of the world's preventable diseases are found.[49] This evocative statistic was one of a number of factors that led to a scaling up of research into relatively neglected conditions.

Research, initially, is lab-based, using test tube and then animal studies. But there comes a point where potential new therapies must be tested in human populations, first on a small scale for safety, and then on a larger scale for efficacy, through various phases. For several reasons these drug trials are now often conducted in developing countries. First, if a new therapy to address the 10/90 gap is discovered, it must be tested in the setting where the condition occurs. Second, if a treatment is proposed that is known to be effective elsewhere, it must be retested in the new environment, especially in populations with different genetic profiles.[50] Finally, in some tension with the previous reasoning, therapies designed for the developed world are also tested in developing world settings, both for financial reasons and because often regulations are less restrictive. In addition to this, there are also what can be thought of as pure research projects, in which no drugs are tested.

It was, indeed, a notorious example of a pure research project that ushered in the new age of research ethics: the Tuskegee Syphilis Study in Alabama, conducted by the U.S. Public Health Service from 1932 to 1972. About 600 African American men, mostly sharecroppers, four hundred with syphilis, were followed so that the researchers could find out more about the natural course of the disease. When a cheap cure became available in 1947—penicillin—it was not offered to the subjects as it would have ruined the study. The experiment ended in 1972 when the press uncovered the story and it became front-page news.[51] Chillingly, it has recently been discovered that the US Public Health Service undertook a similarly unethical project in Guatemala in the 1940s, where 700 people were deliberately infected with syphilis and other sexually transmitted diseases to see if penicillin, if used immediately after sex, could prevent transmission. The research subjects were not told the nature of the experiment or asked to consent, and the results were never published.[52]

Of course, the Tuskegee experiment was not the first known example of deeply unethical research in the twentieth century.[53] The Nazi doctors, tried at Nuremberg, experimented on concentration camp inmates at Dachau and elsewhere, by, for example subjecting people to extreme cold temperatures, observing the effects of hypothermia, and trying out different methods of

rewarming. The purpose of the research, in which many subjects died, was to be able to provide the best response for German pilots shot down over the North Sea.[54] These experiments
led, ultimately, to the World Health Assembly Helsinki Declaration of 1964, amended several times since, regulating scientific
research on human subjects. The declaration puts the idea of
informed consent at center stage.[55] Yet the Tuskegee experiment
carried on even past the Helsinki Declaration.

It is, of course, one thing to have a protocol to govern the ethics of experiments. It is another for scientists to be fully attuned
to all the ethical issues that can arise in relation to research,
and sensitivities can be much higher when the research takes
place in the developing world. The Nuffield Council on Bioethics set out four issues where ethical concerns—and potential
human rights abuses—arise in connection with medical research
in developing countries.[56] Although distinct, we will see, in
fact, that they are all related. First, the gold standard of ethical
research is informed consent. This can be fraught with difficulties. Some people entering the trial may not really absorb the
fact that a trial has two "arms": one that will receive the treatment and the other, the control, which will receive something
else, either a placebo or an existing treatment. If assigned to the
control arm, they may feel they have been tricked into the trial.
There are also questions about who has the right to consent. In
Western trials only the individual subject has the capacity, but
in some traditional societies women are expected to do what
their husbands or elders instruct. Still, there may be imaginative
ways around this problem.

A second problem concerns the review of research ethics
in the country concerned. In the developed world, research
on human subjects must first undergo rigorous ethical investigation. The developing world has had to catch up, and a

concern can be that ethics committees do not always have the political might to question proposals from powerful interests. However, funders are increasingly insisting on local ethical review, and so this seems to be a matter that over time is being addressed.

The third and fourth problems are much more difficult. These are the problems of "what happens after the trial?" and "standard of care," the latter of which came to international attention in 1997 as a result of publicity given to a series of HIV trials in several developing countries. The purpose was to explore transmission of HIV from mothers to infants. By this time it was understood that a dose of Zidovudine (AZT) administered to a mother could reduce the likelihood of transmission. However, there was a question as to what the optimum dose should be and a hypothesis was formed that a lower dose than customary could also be equally effective. If so, this could allow much wider treatment without increasing costs and, perhaps, reducing the chance of side effects, and so the question was an important one. The experimenters followed normal protocol for a randomized clinical trial, assigning a group of patients to the experimental arm and a group to the control arm. The controversial element was what those in the control arm should be given.

Standard experimental procedure, following the Helsinki Declaration, states that the control arm should be offered the best currently available standard of care. One argument is that the best current standard of care was to offer the high dose of Zidovudine. Instead, the control arm received only a placebo. The experimenters' defense was that these patients would not, in the ordinary context of the health systems of the countries in which the research was conducted, have received any treatment, and hence a placebo was equivalent to the best local standard of care: nothing. Several ethics committees agreed. Yet in a famous critique, Lurie and Wolfe decry the double standard of this approach. Research that would have been condemned as unethical if conducted in the United States (because of the local standard of care) is somehow declared ethical in the developing world. As Lurie and Wolfe argue, "Residents of impoverished, post-colonial countries, the majority of which are people of color, must be protected from potential exploitation in research. Otherwise, the abominable state of health care in these countries can be used to justify studies that would never pass muster in the sponsoring country."[57]

In defense, it might be said that applying US standards to the developing world and providing the standard dose of AZT to mothers in the control arm would have been prohibitively expensive, and so the research simply could not have been done. Lurie and Wolfe contend that the manufacturers would have donated the drug free of charge for the trial, and so although cost can be relevant—for example if a coronary care unit had to be built—in this case it was not. Why, then, did the researchers insist on a placebo? Apparently, because they believed that this would make the study scientifically more powerful. This decision probably cost the lives of hundreds of infants. If this is correct, it seems a clear violation of the Helsinki Declaration, which requires the researchers never to put the interests of science over the interests of the participants. Thus it was a violation of the right to health of the participants, even if they would never have received treatment without the trial.

It seems that the Lurie and Wolfe article, as well as the editorial by Marcia Angell in the same edition of *The New England Journal of Medicine*, was a wake-up call to researchers. Although other trials conducted at around that time were also criticized (for example, a trial in Uganda looking at the susceptibility of HIV patients to TB),[58] it seems that the critics have won the argument that the "best existing standard of care" for the control arm of a randomized control trial cannot be interpreted as "best local standard of care," unless the cost is prohibitive or other exceptional circumstances apply. And there can be exceptional circumstances. For example, the Nuffield Council suggest that sometimes using the "universal" standard of care will provide research results that are not relevant to the health care needs of the country where the research is undertaken.[59] Indeed, in criticism of Marcia Angell, Solomon Benatar has suggested that in the very HIV trials that caused the controversy it may not have been appropriate to use the standard of care demanded by the critics, for the full standard of care to prevent mother-to-child transmission of HIV involves replacing breast feeding with bottle feeding, and in much of the developing world this is a very serious health risk to infants.[60] When we start to think of cases like this we can see that exceptional circumstances are, in fact, rather commonplace, and the cut-and-dried certainty of Lurie and Wolfe and Marcia Angell does not do justice to the complexities.

Even more difficult is the question of what happens once the trial is over. This is not a central issue in the case discussed by Lurie and Wolfe, as it was the test of a short-course treatment to prevent mother-to-child transmission, and, at least in relation to the experiment, follow-up treatment is not directly relevant. However, in many trials a treatment is given for a chronic condition to see if any benefit is observed. Suppose such a trial takes place, and the experimental arm shows significant improvements over the control arm; hence the experiment is a success. For scientific purposes, at that point the experimenters can pack up and go home, but there is an argument that they have an ethical obligation to continue the treatment for the experimental arm and to introduce it for the control arm.

After all, the results would not have been possible without the cooperation, at some risk, of all of these people, and extensive obligations have been acquired. Accordingly, it is reasonable to insist that all participants should benefit from research.

However, there is the question of what form that benefit should take. For example, is payment enough to discharge other obligations? Or simply participation even in the control arm of the trial, which generally offers access to other forms of health care for the duration of the trial?[61] Not, apparently, according to the version of the Helsinki Declaration adopted in 2000, Section 30 of which states: "At the conclusion of the study, every patient entered into the study should be assured of access to the best proven prophylactic, diagnostic and therapeutic methods identified by the study."[62] Is this a reasonable demand? In some cases, such as some successful vaccine trials, it would seem highly negligent to ignore it. And withdrawing treatment can be very harmful; for example, if this would encourage the development of drug-resistant strains of a virus. But can these examples be generalized?

Where a medical trial is undertaken to research therapies for chronic conditions, continued treatment for all is an open-ended, and potentially very expensive, commitment. It would be even worse if the trial shows only modest benefits for a very expensive drug. Should every participant be provided with this drug for the rest of their lives, even though it would not pass a test for cost-effectiveness? Or is this simply the price a sponsor must pay for conducting research? The Nuffield Council notes:

> If sponsors of research were required to fund the future provision of interventions shown to be effective to research participants or the wider community, many would cease to support such research. Sponsors from the public sector, such as the UK

MRC or US NIH, would simply be unable to bear the costs involved without curtailing other research. Although the financial resources of many pharmaceutical companies are large, many of them would be equally reluctant to take on the additional burden of long-term commitment.[63]

A recent controversy concerns trials to test preventative interventions for HIV, such as male circumcision, or behavioral interventions. Inevitably in these trials some people will be HIV-negative at the start of the trial but will seroconvert, as it is put, and end up HIV-positive, by the end of the trial. No preventative intervention will be totally effective, and for the control arm no intervention was offered in any case. Should those who become infected during the trial receive treatment?[64] This could be a huge commitment given the size of some trials, and, as the Nuffield Council indicates, the costs could be enough to deter researchers from undertaking such a project.

It may seem more helpful to put matters the other way round. If it is not possible to offer, even to the participants, the benefits of a successful trial, this should raise alarm bells. Perhaps the inability to offer continued treatment simply reveals that the trial was, all along, unethical, in not meeting local health care needs. Indeed, including the condition of post-trial access to health care will be a way of ensuring that a trial in a developing country is not simply the next stage up from an animal trial. Research in developing countries is not to be undertaken lightly, and built into the trial should be a plan for treatment follow-up, if appropriate, whether with local health care providers or external donors. Otherwise the trial runs the danger of exploiting vulnerable communities.[65]

But to insist on such a hard and fast rule is problematic. First, there may be a significant time lag between a trial and the technical possibility of rolling out treatment, even if that is the full intention. Second, it is not uncommon for what was initially thought to be not cost-effective to become so, if, for example, drug companies can be persuaded to donate drugs or donors to fund them.[66] This is an argument that Paul Farmer has made over and over again. What is and is not affordable very often depends on pricing decisions, which are made by humans and not facts of nature. A successful trial can make the difference in persuasion. Therefore, there can be strategically beneficial reasons for conducting a trial, even if extending the benefits is at the present time unaffordable. In fact, work of this type is one of the most important developments in extending access to expensive treatments.

Less encouragingly, though, there can be movement in the other direction: what might have been thought to be affordable is found to be unaffordable. The Nuffield Council reports the following depressing tale:

> Although a successful national trial of bed-nets treated with insecticide in The Gambia reduced overall child mortality from malaria by approximately 30%, it was decided by the researchers, sponsors and the Gambian Ministry of Health that when the research was implemented nationally the cost of the insecticide would have to be recovered because the Ministry could not afford to provide free insecticide indefinitely. Charging for insecticide led to a reduction in the number of young children sleeping under an insecticide-treated net from around 70% to 20%.[67]

Here we see, once more, the clash between progressive realization and core obligations. Under the view of progressive realization, it is not a violation of the right to health of these children not to provide insecticide, for resource constraints are so tight that it is not possible for the government to satisfy the demand.

Alternatively, it could be argued that keeping children malaria-free by a cheap and simple means is a core obligation, and hence the duty of the government is to seek external resources to support the program. And it would be a duty of the world community to meet the need.

Yet we always have to be on the lookout for unintended consequences. In a discussion with a treasury official in Namibia, I asked whether the government was supplying free treated nets to children in the vulnerable areas in the north of the country. I was told that they had tried to interest outside parties to help and received an offer from a donor to supply imported treated bed nets. However, Namibia already had a manufacturer of bed nets producing them at below the cost of the imported nets. The government was reluctant to accept the offer of free nets as it would be likely to put their domestic producer out of business, and in a year or two, when the donor had lost interest, their cheap supply of local nets would no longer be available. Accordingly, the government asked for money to purchase nets from the local supplier. But the donor was not interested. Some people then criticized the Namibian officials for refusing the offer of free help. Obtaining the right sort of external assistance to meet a country's human rights obligations is rarely straightforward.

MATERNAL MORTALITY AND NEWBORN SURVIVAL

One fascinating thing about human rights is that while the general idea of human rights has strong support, very often particular claims that human rights are being violated are treated with irritation, even contempt. In the UK, for example, it is sometimes thought that European human rights legislation is exploited by asylum seekers or prisoners to gain undeserved privileges. From time to time politicians argue that something has gone wrong with a system in which human rights are unpopular. In fact, unpopularity is exactly what we should expect. The whole point of human rights is to protect the marginalized, oppressed, or excluded from the tyranny of common discriminatory or oppressive practices. Broadly, human rights wouldn't be needed if claims made in terms of human rights were easily accepted.

Having said that, not all human rights claims need be unpopular. In some cases they simply point out that a series of decisions, policies, actions, or, indeed, inactions, turn out to have a set of unintended consequences that cannot be tolerated. Consider the shocking facts about maternal and newborn survival in much of the developing world. It is not easy to be sure of figures here, as those who are most at risk are members of highly excluded populations where record collecting is very imperfect, but nevertheless estimates have been made and are extraordinary. Here are some widely cited figures, from a joint statement by the WHO, UNFPA, UNICEF, and the World Bank in 2008:

> Every minute a woman dies in pregnancy or childbirth, over 500,000 every year. And every year over one million newborns die within their first 24 hours of life for lack of quality care. Maternal mortality is the largest health inequity in the world; 99 per cent of maternal deaths occur in developing countries— half of them in Africa. A woman in Niger faces a 1 in 7 chance during her lifetime of dying of pregnancy-related causes, while a woman in Sweden has 1 chance in 17,400.[68]

How are these women and newborns dying? "Women in developing countries are bleeding to death after giving birth, writhing in the convulsions of eclampsia, and collapsing from days of futile contractions, knowing that they have suffocated their babies to death."[69] Yet until very recently maternal mortality attracted relatively little attention, compared, say, to the major infectious diseases. This is not to say that it has been ignored entirely. Number five of the Millennium Development Goals set out by the UN in 2000 was "Reduce by three-quarters, between 1990 and 2015, the maternal mortality ratio." This required year-on-year improvement of 5.5 percent between 2000 and 2015. In 2009 the UN put out a statement on maternal mortality and human rights acknowledging the scale of the problem and the very unimpressive pace of improvement to date: 1 percent per year.[70]

Why has the world been so slow to think of maternal mortality as a health crisis, and so ineffective in dealing with it? For one thing it is not new; it has always been part of the human condition, and poor communities may have grown used to the idea that a significant proportion of women will die in childbirth. Sexism and fatalism have a powerful numbing effect. For another, maternal mortality is not glamorous. This is not to say that suffering from HIV/AIDS is glamorous, but HIV is the type of condition for which a major technological advance may be possible. There are Nobel Prizes, knighthoods, and congressional medals at stake. Funders are in a competitive race to seek a cure. A breakthrough in the lab could save millions of people and make billions of dollars. But there is no pill or vaccine to end maternal mortality. Indeed, we already have the knowledge we need to bring down the numbers of deaths dramatically. The contributors to maternal mortality are lack of prenatal care, of skilled birth attendants, and of basic health facilities such as blood banks, together with very poor rural transport infrastructure, user fees both official and through bribery and corruption, and a whole host of other mundane facts of grinding hardship. As Amnesty International put it: "Maternal mortality reflects the cycle of human rights abuse—deprivation, exclusion, insecurity and voicelessness—that defines and perpetuates poverty."[71]

What this picture misses, though, is that relieving poverty is not enough to tackle maternal mortality. It is one of the few areas where improvements in overcoming poverty—improved nutrition, improved female literacy, improved housing conditions—make relatively little difference on their own. In previous centuries, members of royal families died in childbirth as well as the peasant women on their estates. Maternal complications are brutely physical, and the basic underlying conditions, such as hemorrhage and sepsis, can be found in similar proportions throughout the world and throughout history. The great majority of birth complications cannot be predicted or prevented. What differs is our ability to react to problems when they occur. Almost all can be treated, if accessible medical services are in place. And there lies the problem.[72]

In this respect maternal mortality importantly contrasts with child (as distinct from newborn) mortality. The WHO reports that in 2008 8.8 million children died from preventable diseases before the age of five. Many of these deaths occurred in countries with large populations: China, India, Nigeria, Pakistan, the Democratic Republic of Congo, and Ethiopia. But this masks the fact that the highest rates, as distinct from total numbers, are in countries that have recently been through civil war, where massive displacement of peoples, breakup of family structure, rape, and neglect create a health crisis which makes young children especially vulnerable. Such countries include Angola, Sierra Leone, Liberia, and, once more, the Democratic Republic of Congo.[73] A teenage mother living in an unsanitary, overcrowded refugee camp, with little medical help and no mother, aunts, or village healers to support her, will struggle to keep her children alive. In the worst cases, one in four children do not survive.

The remedies for child death are mostly a matter of prevention or simple cure. Rarely is emergency treatment essential: the fatal condition normally could easily have been prevented. The situation is the reverse for maternal mortality. Some prevention is possible—diagnosis of pre-eclampsia is one area—but on the whole the key to maternal survival is medical: quick and effective intervention if a complication arises, and access to safe abortion. The government's human rights responsibility cannot be to eliminate all maternal deaths, for sadly this cannot be achieved. Rather, it is to create a structure in which good-quality obstetric services are in place, and UN guidelines exist by which this can be monitored.[74]

Countries where rates of maternal mortality are high are failing to protect and fulfill the human right to health of women and their children. Yet making significant inroads will be incredibly expensive, simply because it is a question of providing quality medical and transport infrastructure. Of course there are different ways in which money can be spent. A country that decides to put its money into high-tech hospitals in the capital city, rather than training midwives in rural areas, may have made decisions that cut against its human rights duties, but even had it spent its meager resources more efficiently it will not solve the problem. To meet their core obligations, many of the countries of the world need external assistance. It becomes our problem too. What can be done? There is, at last, major international attention to this scandalous situation. Amnesty International has started a campaign called Demand Dignity; Sarah Brown, wife of former UK prime minister Gordon Brown, is Patron of the White Ribbon Alliance for Safe Motherhood; and other organizations are now scaling up their public profile and fund-raising initiatives.

However, as observed by Arial Frisancho from the International Initiative on Maternal Mortality and Human Rights, work is also needed on the "demand side." Not only is it necessary for medical facilities to be made available; women have to be prepared to use them. There may be cultural barriers to access—the role of traditional birth attendants, fear of authority, concern about being away from families—as well as financial issues of cost that need to be addressed, in addition to the provision of facilities. Cultural sensitivity—for example, allowing women to give birth in traditional ways, such as standing supported rather than lying on a hospital bed—is crucially important. Soyata Maïga, the Special Rapporteur on the Rights of Women in Africa, noted that "Women do not go to the health center because they're too far and doctors don't speak our language and in our culture, women cannot take their clothes off in front of men who are not their husbands."[75] This brings to mind the insistence in General Comment 14 that medical provision must be "culturally appropriate." But perhaps even more important is overcoming entrenched forms of discrimination, in which death in childbirth is largely taken for granted and barely noticed. Despite claims that we know how to avoid most of the world's maternal mortality, it is not an easy matter to bring this about. Progress is there, but it needs rapid acceleration.

CONCLUSION

There are many obstacles to the fulfillment of the human right to the highest attainable standard of health for all. Progress in other areas, such as economic development or copyright harmonization, can, we have seen, create new barriers too. We saw in chapter 2 that there are also worries that approaching health in terms of human rights can be damaging, siphoning money and resources away from more cost-effective approaches to health, replacing rational planning with allocation to the most litigious. This can happen. A government under pressure to fund an HIV/AIDS treatment program may have to cut other forms of spending, or eat into the education or transport budget. On the other hand, through the case studies in this and the previous chapter we have also seen something rather different. Instead of diverting resources away from other health areas, human right to health campaigns can bring new resources into the health sector. If drug companies are pressured into lowering their prices in the developing world and still make a modest profit, then everyone wins. Even if they take a small loss, it will be felt by their shareholders and not other parts of the health system. Similarly, private donors, motivated by energetic and persuasive human right to health campaigns, provide money that might otherwise have sat in their bank accounts or have been used for luxury consumption. Economists emphasize the idea of opportunity cost: if you spend money one way, then it is not available to spend another way. Although this must be true, at least in the short term, it is a very static, and rather dispiriting, view of the world. Spending money on health can create real benefits that also generate, or at least save, money in the future, by, for example, allowing people to return to work and to live long enough to bring their children up in a loving and safe environment. In any case, and this is the main point, a highly focused and well-thought-out human right to health campaign is likely to bring new resources to the developing world, and not simply divert resources from other health priorities. Problems will always be with us—think of the internal brain drain—but to be aware of the dangers is the first step toward avoiding them.

Chapter 5

WHERE NEXT?

EMERGING CAMPAIGNS

In the last chapter we looked at a number of issues where critics of international institutions and practices raised acute concerns about practices that undermined countries' abilities to meet their human rights duties, or did little or nothing to help them meet their core obligations. The examples discussed were all cases where a deficit was noted and action, eventually, was taken, albeit often with slower results than one might have hoped. There remain, however, major health rights challenges of which the world is only just beginning to take notice.

One is mental health, which the WHO has recently focused on as a human rights issue, pointing out that it is very often the case that people suffering from mental health problems have other human rights violated, either through government action, such as forced incarceration, or through social stigma and the violence of others, including the "therapeutic violence" of forced exorcism, for example. And many citizens face mental health challenges as a result of other human rights abuses, most notably torture, rape, and forced migration. As one author noted in 1995, "After three decades of dictatorships, Africa has become a gigantic asylum for victims of torture and repression."[1] Poor African countries may seem to lack the resources to do much for those with mental health difficulties. Still, notice has been taken. *The Lancet* produced an important series of papers on global mental health in 2007 and the WHO has now taken it on as a major concern, issuing guidance in various forms and declaring October 11, 2011, World Mental Health Day. The WHO argues that with the right policies both pharmaceutical and community-based treatment is possible on a global scale. In fact, a concern for mental health was present from the start at the WHO, in its definition of health as a "complete state of physical, mental and social well-being." Indeed, the first director-general of the WHO, Canadian George Brock Chisholm, was a psychiatrist. But mental health faded from view as a global health issue until recently. Addressing mental health in any significant fashion has yet to be achieved.

There are, of course, many other major global health issues coming to prominence. One is the penetration of Western "lifestyle" conditions in low- and middle-income countries, ranging from diabetes to road traffic accidents, now one of the major causes of death in middle-income countries. Another major source of death through accidents is the large number of drownings, especially for children and teenage boys, by either pure accident, fishing, floods, or tsunamis. If the pattern noticed here is followed for these conditions, we will see NGOs gaining publicity for a cause, followed by a report by the WHO (which is the stage we are at for the conditions mentioned here), followed by action by a donor, government or multilateral agency, which will then be criticized (fairly or unfairly) for its ineffectiveness, arrogance, and cultural insensitivity but then used as a model for a large-scale intervention program. The question is, how can we make progress while avoiding the mistakes of the last two decades?

GOVERNANCE AND ACTIVISM

Without supposing that it is possible to know the answers, it is worth pointing to several areas of concern that have been highlighted in the academic literature, showing how improvements may strengthen governments' ability to meet their human right to health obligations in the future.

The first is, no doubt, the dullest: data. Report after report points out that it is very hard to get a grip on the facts because basic data is missing. Even birth, marriage, and death data is not regularly collected everywhere. The WHO Commission on the Social Determinants of Health, the *Lancet* report on the human right to health, and the WHO study on maternal mortality are just some of the many reports that complain that vital data is absent, and that this has impeded their work. And so, it is said, more resources need to be devoted to data collection. Those outside academia may be suspicious of this claim, noting that those who make their living through research are bound to argue that more research is needed. If there is a choice between spending money to save lives and spending money to collect data, it is not difficult to see where we should spend it. But the natural response is that this is a false dilemma. We need to spend money to find out where money needs to be spent. In particular, from a human rights point of view, we need disaggregated data.

For example, life expectancy in Australia is among the highest in the world, which could lead one to think that there is no health crisis. But life expectancy for aboriginal Australians is about twenty years lower than for those of European descent. And then we need to know why this is. Is it that it is rare for aboriginal Australians to reach old age, or is that that there is an excess of infant, childhood, or young adult deaths that brings down the average? Only when data at this level of detail is collected will facts about discrimination, exclusion, and disadvantage jump out. Human rights activism starts with monitoring: the collection of data. Independent monitoring and evaluation of interventions is also vital. After all, anyone running a program will naturally engage in wishful thinking and report to all what a great success it has been, even if it isn't. Without money for quality evaluation, we are working in the dark.

Data collection is one problem; another is "global health governance." A small number of very large organizations, such as the WHO, PEPFAR, the Gates Foundation, GAVI, the Global Fund, and some government-sponsored agencies, as well as perhaps hundreds of thousands of small and medium-sized organizations, all compete to make an impact on human health. How can large organizations—especially large charitable organizations—be held to account?

Consider some recent criticisms of the Gates Foundation. In one way it seems inappropriate, even a matter of poor taste or judgment, to make any criticisms at all. After all, Bill and Melinda Gates could have chosen any way to spend their money, as could Warren Buffett, another major funder of the foundation. Instead, they have made a huge investment in global health. What can be wrong with that? The general problem, so it is claimed, is that the trust's financial power gives them huge influence over the research now conducted and the health problems that receive attention, and this can be problematic. One commentator claims that the Gates Foundation has an excessive focus on technological solutions, such as discovering vaccines, which, we might add, can lead to an "all or nothing" approach. Suppose billions are spent looking for a vaccine for malaria but it turns out unsuccessful. It could be that there is literally nothing to show for all this money, and indeed the scientists who spent their time on this research have been diverted from other tasks that might have been more fruitful.

It is also said that the Gates Foundation's support of vertical programs undermines health systems by encouraging the internal brain drain, and that its enthusiasm for its programs leads it to sometimes bypass ministries of health, thereby undermining the local health system. In sum:

> Although Bill Gates' annual letter indicates a genuine desire of the foundation to help the poor and to do good, further independent research and assessment is needed to ensure that this desire is translated into the right and most cost-effective set of approaches, strategies, and investments for improving the health of the poor.[2]

To give more detailed examples, two of the major Gates priorities have recently been questioned. Elizabeth Pisani has asked whether the Gates initiative to eradicate polio in the next two years is the right priority. A huge effort is being put into dealing with a disease that now affects only a relatively small number of people each year, while other much more significant diseases do not attract funding in anything like a similar proportion. Taking the final step in eradication is very difficult and expensive, and, it is argued, much more good could be done by spending the money on sanitation and clean water.[3] Yet if the money is tied to polio eradication programs, that is how it will have to be spent.

Criticisms have also been voiced, this time by the editor of *The Lancet*, Richard Horton, in a book review in the *New York Review of Books*, concerning the Gates Foundation's proposal to eliminate malaria. On the one hand Horton applauds the grand ambition of this project, noting the huge success that can be achieved by impossible dreamers, who as Bill Shore, author of the book under review, notes, have "irrational self-confidence." Malaria, after all, was endemic in the United States until as recently as 1951. Horton makes a distinction between eradication—the removal of the malaria parasite from the planet—and elimination: taking measures within a country or region that ensure there are no infections. Elimination in certain parts of the world, those with better health systems, is possible, argues Horton, but the goal of eradication is, he thinks, naive and not feasible, at least within the next fifty years or so.[4] If the failure of eradication is predictable then the money spent on it is largely wasted, and would save many more lives through control and elimination. If the project was run by the WHO there are forms of governance that would steer the funding, eventually, to what can be supported by the best evidence. But the money is under the control of Gates, and he, roughly speaking, can do what he likes. He is able to recruit many of the world's premier scientists to try to achieve his ambition. In the medium term this could do far more harm than good, by diverting them from more modest but more achievable goals.

The issues of governance we have illustrated so far concern "top-down" organization and direction. Many activists in global health seek "bottom-up" approaches to health, where those who will benefit from treatment or interventions are involved not only in campaigning for change but also in control of their conditions, and in the future direction of research. People should not be "patients," but be empowered to take control of their own fates. We saw this demand illustrated in the case of HIV, through the initial enunciation of the Denver Principles and in the application of American-style activism to the situation in South Africa by the Treatment Action Campaign. The slogan of the disability movement—"nothing about us without us"—sums up this approach.

But how extensive is the grassroots movement for health? And what are its prospects? In relation to the human right to health this is a particular concern, for if human rights activism cannot marshal and interact with a broad base it will be the preserve of the wealthy and well-connected. Paul Farmer quotes exactly this line of thought from Chidi Anselm Odinkalu's "Why More Africans Don't Use Human Rights Language":

Most human rights organizations are modelled after Northern watchdog organizations, located in an urban area, run by a core management, without a membership base (unlike Amnesty International) and dependent solely on overseas funding. The most successful of these organizations only manage to achieve the equivalent status of a public policy think-tank, a research institute or a specialized publishing house. With media-driven visibility and a lifestyle to match, the leaders of these initiatives enjoy privilege and comfort, and progressively grow distant from a life of struggle.

In the absence of a membership base there is no constituency-driven obligation or framework for popularizing the language or objectives of the group beyond the community of inward-looking careerists who run it. Instead of being the currency of a social justice or conscience-driven movement, "human rights" has increasingly become the specialized language of a select cadre with its own rites of passage and methods of certification. Far from being a badge of honor, human rights activism is, in some of the places I have observed it, increasingly a sign of privilege.[5]

The accuracy of this observation has to be acknowledged. Just as there was a time when everyone who was anyone in New York had to have their own AIDS charity, now being part of a human rights campaign may have the same social cachet. Surely few people think this is a desirable state of affairs, but what can be done about it? The broad-based People's Health Movement aims to do better. It claims to have "roots deep in the grassroots people's movement and owes its genesis to many health networks and activists who have been concerned by the growing inequities in health over the last 25 years."[6] In practice, of course, it will be very hard to build a popular movement for health that captures people who are not academics, health workers, NGO activists, or those campaigning on a particular health issue that affects them or their family or friends. Who cares about health unless you earn your living that way or are ill? But the aspirations are right, and the People's Health Movement reaches across the globe, setting out its goals in a People's Health Charter and being a major sponsor of the Global Health Watch Reports, billed as an "alternative world health report," which were published in 2006 and 2009, with a third in preparation. Pressure is building, even if progress can be painfully slow. And everyone can find a role.

CONCLUSION

We began, in the introduction, by setting out a dilemma. On the one hand the state of global health provides an apparently compelling case for a universal human right to health. On the other hand, especially considering the resource implications, the idea of such a right seems utterly unrealistic. Many theorists and practitioners have, for this reason, argued against approaching global health through a rights framework and instead propose that we look for cost-effective approaches to health given the budgets at our disposal. Others insist that we must recognize the human right to health and find ways of making it realistic. Often this comes down to a matter of making the unaffordable affordable, and that can often be achieved by creating a secure alliance between drug companies, donors, and international organizations. Paul Farmer is one of the people who has taken the lead on this approach, refusing to compromise and even using the idea of the human right to health as leverage in persuading powerful actors to find ways of doing the right thing. Progress may have been slow, but as we have seen in previous chapters there is a model for action. Of course, there are many gaps. We don't know how to cure everything, and there are stubborn problems, such as maternal mortality, where the Farmer solution of providing a cheap model will not be enough. Rural women will continue to die in childbirth if the transport infrastructure is too poor to allow them to get to the emergency clinic in time. No single actor has it in their power to change this. Still, this is no reason to give up the struggle, or to give up the human right of every mother to safe conditions of childbirth, as part of the human right to the highest attainable standard of health.

The human right to health made its first appearance in international law in the Universal Declaration of Human Rights in 1948, in the guise of the right to medical care. In 1954 it was extended to the right "to the enjoyment of the highest attainable standard of physical and mental health" by means of the

Covenant on Economic, Social, and Cultural Rights. However it did not become binding until the ratification of the covenant in 1976. Two years later, the declaration of Alma-Ata, often regarded as the most important moment in the development of the human right to health, reaffirmed and extended the right to health, placing it in the context of its social and economic determinants.

At every stage the human right to health has had to battle against skepticism, whether general skepticism about whether there are any human rights, or a more specific skepticism about whether health itself can be a human right. In abstract terms it can be easy to lose one's grip on what the right to health could be. It is somehow more than the right to medical care, but less than the right to be healthy. But when we turn to concrete cases, it doesn't seem quite so difficult to understand.

Indeed, as has been argued here, the idea of the human right to health began to find real use in relation to HIV/AIDS in late 1980s. By the mid-1990s it was receiving increasing attention, and, it can be argued, reached international maturity with the issuance of General Comment 14 in 2000, the appointment of a Special Rapporteur in 2002, and a series of developments in 2003 including Nelson Mandela's assertion that AIDS had become a human rights issue. It was made respectable, perhaps, to the medical community by *The Lancet*'s report on the right to health in 194 countries in 2008. It seems that the human right to health is here, and is likely to be here to stay. While it still has its critics, this can only be a good thing, both to guard against complacency and to allow theorists, activists, health professionals and governments to continue to influence the development of what is still a living, breathing, hugely important work in progress.

NOTES

Introduction: The Human Right to Health Dilemma

1. Amartya Sen, foreword to Paul Farmer, *Pathologies of Power* (Berkeley: University of California Press, 2005).
2. World Bank, *Investing in Health: The World Development Report for 1993* (Oxford: Oxford University Press, 1993), 200. Available online at: http://files.dcp2.org/pdf/WorldDevelopmentReport1993.pdf.
3. Lawyers have argued that there is another serious difficulty: that the right is not "justiciable," or, in other words, capable of being used in legal actions. For an important rebuttal of this criticism, by looking in detail at how the human right to health has in fact been used in courts in five different countries, see Varun Gauri and Dan Brinks, eds., *Courting Social Justice* (Cambridge: Cambridge University Press, 2008).

Chapter 1: The Universal Declaration of Human Rights

1. This is not to say that the weather never gives rise to questions about human rights. Consider, for example, climate change caused by human action.
2. The account of Moleen Mudimu is told in Stephanie Nolen, *28 Stories of AIDS in Africa* (London: Portobello Books, 2007), 321–31 and 375–76.
3. Farmer, *Pathologies of Power*.
4. United Nations, *International Covenant on Economic, Social and Cultural*

Rights (1966). Available online at: http://www2.ohchr.org/english/law/cescr.htm.

5. United Nations, *Universal Declaration of Human Rights* (1948). Available online at: http://www.un.org/en/documents/udhr/.

6. The origin and drafting of the UDHR is a fascinating story, beautifully told in two highly contrasting books on which I rely here: Mary Ann Glendon's *A World Made New: Eleanor Roosevelt and the Universal Declaration of Human Rights* (New York: Random House, 2001) and Johannes Morsink's *The Universal Declaration of Human Rights: Origins, Drafting and Intent* (Philadelphia: University of Pennsylvania Press, 1999). Glendon blends together the drafting and development of the Declaration with biographical accounts especially of Eleanor Roosevelt, but also other key figures such as Charles Malik, René Cassin, Peng-chun Chang, and John Humphrey. These people also feature heavily in Morsink's scholarly work, yet his task is to explain, by painstaking reference, especially to committee minutes, how more or less every phrase, almost every word, in the declaration came to earn its place. The patience, tenacity, and legal and philosophical talent of the key group of drafters was remarkable. The process gives the lie to a common criticism made of the Declaration—that it was poorly or hastily drafted. Of course there are unclarities, but for a document drafted by a series of committees it is hugely impressive.

7. The four freedoms are memorably illustrated by Norman Rockwell.

8. Glendon, *A World Made New*, 170.

9. World Health Organization, *Chronicle of the World Health Organization* (1947). Available online at: http://whqlibdoc.who.int/hist/chronicles/chronicle_1947.pdf.

10. Ibid., 8.

11. Ibid., 11.

12. World Health Organization, *Constitution* (1946/2006). Available online at: http://www.who.int/governance/eb/who_constitution_en.pdf.

13. United Nations, *UDHR*.

14. There are some significant omissions, including China, Cuba, Burma, Saudi Arabia, and Singapore.

15. United Nations, *ICESCR*.

16. International Conference on Primary Health Care, *Declaration of Alma-Ata* (1978). Available online at: http://www.who.int/hpr/NPH/docs/declaration_almaata.pdf.

17. Indeed, some years later, the WHO formulation of the right was

recognized in the UN Convention on the Rights of the Child, adopted in 1989, and coming into force very soon afterward, in 1990. Article 24(1) reads: "States Parties recognize the right of the child to the enjoyment of the highest attainable standard of health and to facilities for the treatment of illness and rehabilitation of health. States Parties shall strive to ensure that no child is deprived of his or her right of access to such health care services." United Nations, *Convention on the Rights of the Child* (1989). Available online at: http://www2.ohchr.org/english/law/crc.htm. Although, as we noted, ICESCR has not been universally adopted, the position is much more encouraging for the Convention on the Rights of the Child. According to UNICEF, it has been ratified by all countries of the world except Somalia, with no effective government, and the USA, which is always very slow to ratify human rights conventions. (UNICEF, *Convention on the Rights of the Child: Frequently Asked Questions* (2006). Available online at: http://www.unicef.org/crc/index_30229.html.) In consequence, virtually all countries in the world have accepted the right to the highest attainable standard of health for children, and many have accepted it for all their citizens.

18. United Nations, *ICESCR* Article 2(1). See also Kristin Hessler and Allen Buchanan "Specifying the Content of the Human Right to Health Care," in *Medicine and Social Justice: Essays on the Distribution of Health Care*, ed. R. Rhodes, M. Pabst Battin and A. Silvers (Oxford: Oxford University Press, 2002).

19. United Nations, General Comment 14 (2000). Available online at: http://www.unhchr.ch/tbs/doc.nsf/(symbol)/E.C.12.2000.4.En.

20. United Nations, General Comment 3 (1990). Available online at: http://www.unhchr.ch/tbs/doc.nsf/(symbol)/E.C.12.2000.4.En.

21. Other important developments include the appointment in 2002 of Professor Paul Hunt, from the University of Essex in the UK, as first Special Rapporteur on the right to health, to help promote, protect, and advocate for the human right to health, with the obligation to undertake country-based missions and to produce reports. At the end of his term in 2008, Anand Grover, a human rights lawyer specializing in HIV/AIDS litigation, was appointed as second Special Rapporteur.

It is also worth mentioning the optional protocol on ICESCR which was adopted by the General Assembly of the United Nations in 2008 (United Nations, *United Nations Treaty Collection* (2011). Available online at: http://treaties.un.org/Pages/ViewDetails.aspx?

src=TREATY&mtdsg_no=IV-3-a&chapter=4&lang=en). The point of the protocol is to allow individuals to bring their claims to the Committee on Economic, Social, and Cultural Rights for a hearing. At present there is no centralized international forum to which people may make their complaints, although individuals have in some cases had access to domestic courts and to regional courts such as the European Court of Human Rights. However, the committee will only have jurisdiction over those countries that have ratified the protocol, and it will not come into force until ratified by ten states parties. At the time of writing (July 2011) it has been ratified by only three: Ecuador, Mongolia, and Spain. And so it will probably be some considerable time before it enters into force, if it ever does. However, the fact that a new optional protocol has been produced, to fill a clear gap in the existing institutions, shows that human rights law in this area is still evolving, especially under the perception of its own inadequacies. Progress will be slow, but improvements seem possible.

Chapter 2: The Human Right to Health and Its Critics

1. Henry Shue, *Basic Rights*, 2nd ed. (Princeton: Princeton University Press, 1996).
2. It is also sometimes assumed that all first-generation rights are more important than all second-generation rights. Yet this claim has been seriously questioned for decades. As Henry Shue argues, without particular second-generation rights, such as the right to subsistence, many other rights cannot be enjoyed (for one would be dead). Both first- and second-generation rights can be "basic rights" in Shue's terminology (see Shue, *Basic Rights*).
3. Jack Donnelly, "Human Rights and Asian Values: A Defence of 'Western' Universalism," in *The East Asian Challenge For Human Rights*, ed. Joanne R. Bauer and Daniel A. Bell (Cambridge: Cambridge University Press, 1999), 61.
4. Or, for a better documented example, the impressively detailed and thoughtful Namibian development plan Vision 2030 includes the aspiration to move from a country that receives development aid to one that disperses aid to other countries by the year 2030. National Planning Commission of Namibia, *Namibia Vision 2030* (2004). Available online at: http://www.npc.gov.na/vision/vision_2030bgd.htm.

5. For example, it is sometimes said that when Zimbabwe achieved independence the British government assumed that Bishop Abel Muzorewa would be elected prime minister and continue to respect British interests. In fact, his party received very little support from the electorate and the much more radical Robert Mugabe was elected instead.

6. Cited in Glendon, *A World Made New*, 164. It may be hard to understand why the state would be prepared to open itself up to external scrutiny, and we have seen and will see again that many states are very nervous of doing so. However, in the aftermath of the Second World War, when it was becoming clear what Nazi Germany had done to so many of its own citizens, it was hard to argue for the principle of complete internal sovereignty of the state. As philosopher Charles Beitz puts it, human rights exist as an attempt to correct a defect in the way political history has led to the development of the world as a "society of states," each with a concentration of power over its citizens. Human rights doctrine attempts to provide a much-needed counterweight. Charles Beitz, *The Idea of Human Rights* (Oxford: Oxford University Press, 2009), 128–30.

7. Anne-Emanuelle Birn, "Health and Human Rights: Historical Perspectives and Political Challenges," *Journal of Public Health Policy* 29 (2008): 34.

8. For a trenchant presentation of a skeptical position see Bernard Baumrin, "Why There is No Right to Health Care," in *Medicine and Social Justice: Essays on the Distribution of Health Care*, ed. R. Rhodes, M. Pabst Battin, and A. Silvers (Oxford: Oxford University Press, 2002).

9. John Locke, *Two Treatises of Government*, 1689 (Cambridge: Cambridge University Press, 1988).

10. Jeremy Bentham, "Anarchical Fallacies" and "Supply Without Burden," 1796, in *Nonsense Upon Stilts*, ed. Jeremy Waldron (London: Methuen, 1987), 53.

11. Bentham, *Nonsense Upon Stilts*, 72–73. More recently, philosopher Alasdair MacIntyre has twisted the anti-human rights knife: "The best reason for asserting so bluntly that there are no [natural or human] rights is precisely the same type as the best reason we possess for asserting there are no witches [or] unicorns: every attempt to give good reasons for believing that there *are* such rights has failed . . . In the United Nations declaration of 1948 what has since become the normal U.N. practice of not giving good reasons for

any assertions whatsoever is followed with great rigour." Alasdair MacIntyre, *After Virtue* (London: Duckworth, 1981), 67.

12. Jacques Maritain, *Man and the State* (Chicago: University of Chicago Press, 1951), 77.

13. John Rawls, *Political Liberalism* (New York: Columbia University Press, 1993/1996), 135–72.

14. Hessler and Buchanan, "Content of Human Right." Such a proposal fits well with the account of human rights provided by Joseph Raz in "Human Rights Without Foundations," in *The Philosophy of International Law*, ed. J. Tasioulas and S. Besson (Oxford: Oxford University Press, 2010). See also Beitz, *The Idea of Human Rights*. In summary, Raz believes that human rights should now be seen as a branch of international law, and, luckily, a branch of law in reasonably good order. This is essential, Raz argues, if the discussions of philosophers are to engage with the concerns of human rights practice. Seeing matters this way allows us to draw an analogy with other branches of law such as family law or property law. In such cases, the broad contours of the law can be seen as being based on any one of a number of moral reasons, setting limits to what can reasonably be part of the law. So, for example, any reasonable view would wish to give parents duties of care toward their children. Yet it would be unrealistic to think that precise details of maintenance payments for children in case of divorce can be given a philosophical foundation or be the object of a similar consensus. Such issues will be worked out in the practical context of politics and legal casework. The same is possible for the details of human rights. While the overall framework can be justified from a range of philosophical positions, it is not necessary or realistic to think that each particular human right needs a single philosophical justification, or even that the details of its determinate content needs to be acceptable from all points of view.

15. Karl Marx, "On The Jewish Question," 1843, in *Karl Marx: Early Writings*, ed. L. Colletti (Harmondsworth: Penguin, 1975).

16. Onora O'Neill, "The Dark Side of Human Rights," *International Affairs* 81 (2005): 427–39.

17. American Anthropological Association, The Executive Board, "Statement on Human Rights," *American Anthropologist* 49 (1947): 539–40.

18. American Anthropological Association, Committee for Human Rights, *Declaration on Anthropology and Human Rights* (1999). Available online at: http://www.aaanet.org/stmts/humanrts.htm.

19. The drafting committee for the Universal Declaration itself was extremely concerned about the possibility that drawing up a declaration would privilege Western values over others. As the drafters began their business, UNESCO commissioned an investigation into this very topic. A "philosophers' committee," chaired by University of Cambridge historian E. H. Carr, was set up. Questionnaires were sent to leading intellectuals around the world, including Mohandas Gandhi and several other Indian thinkers, and Chinese Confucian philosopher Chung-Shu Lo, as well as Western figures such as Italian philosopher Benedetto Croce and British novelist Aldous Huxley. The questionnaire sought the respondents' views on human rights from a very broad perspective of religious, cultural, and philosophical traditions. The results of the consultation, as Mary Ann Glendon puts it, "were encouraging: they indicated that the principles underlying the draft Declaration were present in many cultural and religious traditions, though not always expressed in terms of rights." Glendon, *A World Made New*, 76.

20. See Donnelly, "Human Rights and Asian Values."

21. In response, it has often been rather smugly pointed out in that it is not clear that Asia is universally hostile to all Western values. After all, several Asian, and indeed African, countries have been enthusiastic champions of another strain of Western values: Marxist communism. However, there remains a prima facie case to answer.

22. Bangkok Declaration (1993). Available online at: http://law.hku.hk/lawgovtsociety/Bangkok%20Declaration.htm.

23. Amartya Sen, *Human Rights and Asian Values* (New York: Carnegie Council on Ethics and International Affairs, 1977), 9, citing W. S. Wong, "The Real World of Human Rights" (mimeographed, 1993).

24. Sen, *Human Rights and Asian Values*, 9–10.

25. We should recall that English philosopher John Locke found himself having to argue against the feudal tradition of the divine right of kings, and as Sen notes it is hard to argue that Plato and Augustine were less authoritarian in sympathy than Confucius. Sen, *Human Rights and Asian Values*, 17.

26. The drafters of the UDHR were well aware of this line of attack—that a statement of states' rights should also be included—frequently raised by the Soviets. In a speech, in his capacity as ambassador of Lebanon, to the US Chamber of Commerce in 1949, Charles Malik eloquently discussed why the Declaration had no place for the rights of states: "The problem of human rights arose in recent

years precisely because society and the state trespassed upon man, to the extent, in totalitarian states, of choking him altogether. In our formulation we are therefore called upon to correct the excesses precisely of statism and socialism. The right amount of anarchism and individualism is exactly what statism and socialism need. It is not that we find ourselves at present in a lawless jungle with every man brutally seeking his own individual advantage without any organized lines of relation and authority; and as a result we are called upon, so to speak, to restore order and authority by reminding men of their duties and obligations: It is rather that we find ourselves today in a situation, all the world over, in which man's simple, essential humanity—his power to laugh and love and think and change his mind, in freedom—is in mortal danger of extinction by reason of endless pressures from every side." Charles Malik, "Talk on Human Rights" (1949), available online at: http://www. udhr.org/history/talkon.htm.

27. Shue, *Basic Rights.*
28. United States Government, *Response to Request* (not dated). Available online at: http://www.globalgovernancewatch.org/docLib/20080213 _US_Hunt_Response.pdf.
29. Gunilla Backman et al., "Health Systems and the Right to Health: An Assessment of 194 Countries," *The Lancet* 372 (2008): 2047–85.
30. It is unclear that incorporating the right to health in the constitution correlates in any significant manner with better health performance in other respects. Few European countries recognize the right to health in domestic law.
31. The authors resist the temptation to present a ranking or league table of countries' performance. In this respect they have probably learned the lesson of the World Health Organization's notorious World Health Report of 2000, *Health Systems: Improving Performance,* which included a "statistical annex" setting out a very controversial ranking of countries, in which France, Italy, San Marino, Andorra, Malta, Singapore, Spain, and Oman occupied the top eight places, with the UK eighteenth, Switzerland twentieth, Sweden twenty-third, Germany twenty-fifth, and the USA thirty-seventh, sandwiched between Costa Rica and Slovenia. Naturally the ranking was used to cast doubt on the methodology, and the exercise, which led to acrimonious dispute within the WHO, has never been repeated, even though the report itself suggests it will be the first of an annual exercise. World Health Organization,

World Health Report: Health Systems: Improving Performance (WHO: Geneva, 2000). Available online at: http://www.who.int/whr/2000/en/whr00_annex_en.pdf.

32. William Easterly, "Human Rights Are the Wrong Basis for Health Care," *Financial Times*, October 12, 2009. Available online at: http://www.ft.com/cms/s/0/89bbbda2-b763-11de-9812-00144feab49a.html.

33. See, for example, William Easterly, *The White Man's Burden* (Oxford: Oxford University Press, 2006).

34. See also S. R. Benatar, "Human Rights in the Biotechnology Era 1," *BMC International Health and Human Rights* 2002: 2: 3.

35. Markus Haacker, "The Macroeconomics of HIV/AIDS," in *Southern Africa: 2020 Vision*, ed. M. Hannam and J. Wolff (London: e9 Publishing, 2010).

36. Anne-Emanuelle Birn, "Health and Human Rights," 32–41.

37. Gilbert Burnham, Riyadh Lafta, Shannon Doocy, and Les Roberts, "Mortality after the 2003 invasion of Iraq: a cross-sectional cluster sample survey," *The Lancet* 368 (2006): 1421–28.

38. Octavio Ferraz, "The Right To Health In The Courts Of Brazil: Worsening Health Inequities?" *Health and Human Rights* 11 (2009) 33–45.

Chapter 3: HIV/AIDS and the Human Right to Health

1. Jonathan M. Mann, "Human Rights and AIDS: The Future of the Pandemic," in *Health and Human Rights*, ed. Jonathan M. Mann, Sofia Gruskin, Michael A. Grodin, and George J. Annas (London: Routledge, 1999), 216.

2. South Africa.Info, "My Son Died of AIDS: Mandela," January 12, 2005, available online at: http://www.southafrica.info/mandela/mandela-son.htm.

3. AVERT "World AIDS Day" 2010, available online at: http://www.avert.org/world-aids-day.htm.

4. Mann, "Human Rights and AIDS," 223. See also George J. Annas, "Human Rights and Health: the Universal Declaration of Human Rights at 50," *New England Journal of Medicine* 339 (1998): 1778–81.

5. Robert C. Gallo, "A Reflection on HIV/AIDS. Research after 25 Years," *Retrovirology* 3 (2006): 72.

6. Peter Baldwin, *Disease and Democracy* (Berkeley: University of California Press, 2005), 27.

7. Paul Farmer, *Aids and Accusation* (Berkeley: University of California Press, 1992).

8. Jonathan M. Mann et al., "Health and Human Rights," in *Health and Human Rights*, ed. Mann et al.

9. David Lush, "Medical Totalitarianism and My Part in Its Downfall," in *Southern Africa*, ed. Hannam and Wolff.

10. Unity Dow and Max Essex, *Saturday is for Funerals* (Cambridge, MA: Harvard University Press, 2008), 216.

11. Baldwin, *Disease and Democracy*.

12. Ibid., 53.

13. Ibid., 52–55.

14. European Court of Human Rights, *Enhorn v. Sweden* (Application no. 56529/00), January 25, 2005.

15. Baldwin, *Disease and Democracy*, 96.

16. Peter Piot, Susan Timberlake, and Jason Sigurdson, "Governance and the Response to AIDS: Lessons for Development and Human Rights," in *Realizing the Right to Health*, ed. Andrew Clapham and Mary Robinson (Zurich: Rüffer & Rub, 2009).

17. Baldwin, *Disease and Democracy*, 191.

18. Ibid., 97.

19. NAPWA, "The Denver Principles 1983 and Today," 2011, available online at: http://www.napwa.org/content/denver-principles-1983-and-today.

20. Baldwin, *Disease and Democracy*, 156.

21. UNAIDS, *The Greater Involvement of People Living With HIV* (GIPA) 2007, available online at: http://data.unaids.org/pub/BriefingNote/2007/jc1299_policy_brief_gipa.pdf.

22. Michael Kirby, "The New AIDS Virus—Ineffective and Unjust Laws," *Journal of Acquired Immune Deficiency Syndromes* 1 (1988): 305.

23. Baldwin, *Disease and Democracy*, 61–62.

24. Mary Crewe, "The HIV/AIDS Epidemic and Human Rights Responses," in *Realizing the Right to Health*, ed. Clapham and Robinson, 278. For an excellent, detailed examination of the ethical dilemmas regarding public health and infection, see Margaret P. Battin, Leslie P. Francis, Jay A. Jacobson, and Charles B. Smith, *The Patient as Victim and Vector: Ethics and Infectious Disease* (Oxford: Oxford University Press, 2009).

25. Mann, "Health and Human Rights," 217.

26. Farmer, *AIDS and Accusation*.

27. Baldwin, *Disease and Democracy.*
28. It is, of course, possible and necessary to treat secondary infections and other conditions, but this does nothing to address the underlying condition.
29. Margaret A. Fischl et al., and the AZT Collaborative Working Group, "The Efficacy of Azidothymidine (AZT) in the Treatment of Patients with AIDS and AIDS-Related Complex," *New England Journal of Medicine* 317 (1987): 185–91.
30. Douglas D. Richman et al., and the AZT Collaborative Working Group, "The Toxicity of Azidothymidine (AZT) in the Treatment of Patients with AIDS and AIDS-Related Complex," *New England Journal of Medicine* 317 (1987): 192–97.
31. E. Dournon et al., "Effects Of Zidovudine In 365 Consecutive Patients With Aids Or Aids-Related Complex," *The Lancet* 332 (1988): 1297–302.
32. Baldwin, *Disease and Democracy*, 223.
33. Ryan White and Ann Marie Cunningham, *My Own Story* (New York: Penguin, 1991).
34. P. W. Eggers, "Medicare's End Stage Renal Disease Program," *Health Care Financing Review* 22 (2000): 55–60.
35. Baldwin, *Disease and Democracy*, 120.
36. Dow and Essex, *Saturday,* 12.
37. AVERT, "HIV and AIDS Treatment in the UK" (2011). Available online at: http://www.avert.org/hiv-treatment-uk.htm.
38. Farmer, *AIDS and Accusation*, 15.
39. Ibid., 2.
40. C. L. R. James, *The Black Jacobins*, 1938 (London: Penguin, 2001).
41. Farmer, *AIDS and Accusation*, 7.
42. Ibid., xii.
43. M. Thomas et al., "The emergence of HIV/AIDS in the Americas and beyond," *Proceedings of the National Academy of Science* 104 (2007): 18566–70.
44. Farmer, *AIDS and Accusation*, 209.
45. Ibid., 216.
46. Ibid., 216.
47. Paul Farmer, *Pathologies of Power* (Berkeley: University of California Press, 2005), 55.
48. George J. Annas, "Detention of HIV-Positive Haitians at Guantánamo," *New England Journal of Medicine* 329 (1993): 592.

49. Quoted in Farmer, *Pathologies*, 66.
50. B. S. Weeks and I. E. Alcamo, *AIDS The Biological Basis*, 5th ed. (Sudbury, MA: Jones and Bartlett, 2010), 13.
51. Zenda Woodman and Carolyn Williamson, "HIV Molecular Epidemiology: Transmission and Adaptation to Human Populations," *Current Opinion in HIV and AIDS* 2009, 4 (2009): 247–52.
52. Gallo, "Reflection on HIV/AIDS Research."
53. Woodman and Williamson, "HIV Molecular Epidemiology."
54. D. Huminer, J. B. Rosenfeld, and S. D. Pitlik, "AIDS in the pre-AIDS era," *Review of Infectious Diseases* 9 (1987): 1102–08.
55. S. S. Frøland et al., "HIV-1 Infection in Norwegian Family before 1970," *The Lancet* 331 (1988): 1344–45.
56. Weeks and Alcoma, *AIDS: The Biological Basis*, 12.
57. Amnesty International, *Uganda: Antihomosexuality Bill Is Inherently Discriminatory And Threatens Broader Human Rights* (London: Amnesty International, 2010).
58. Weeks and Alcoma, *AIDS*, 12.
59. Ibid., xi.
60. L. O. Kallings, "The First Postmodern Pandemic: 25 Years of HIV/AIDS (Review)," *Journal of International Medicine* 263 (2008): 221.
61. Kallings, "The First Postmodern Pandemic," 221; see also Nolen, *28 Stories*.
62. William E. Forbath, "Cultural Transformation, Deep Institutional Reform, and ESR Practice," in *Stones of Hope: African Lawyers Use Human Rights to Challenge Global Poverty*, ed. Jeremy Perelman and Lucie White (Stanford, CA: Stanford University Press, 2011), 51.
63. Daryl Collins, Jonathan Morduch, Stuart Rutherford and Orlanda Ruthven, *Portfolios of the Poor: How the World's Poor Live on $2 a Day* (Princeton: Princeton University Press, 2009), and Dow and Essex, *Saturday*.
64. Rachel Hammonds and Gorik Ooms, "World Bank Policies and the Obligation of its Members to Respect, Protect and Fulfill the Right To Health," *Health and Human Rights* 8 (2004): 26–60.
65. Piot et al., "Governance and the Response to AIDS," 335.
66. Nolen, *28 Stories*, 108.
67. Ibid., 109–11.
68. Kallings, "The First Postmodern Pandemic," 224.
69. United Nations, *Political Declaration on HIV/AIDS*, 2006. Available

online at: http://data.unaids.org/pub/Report/2006/20060615_hlm_politicaldeclaration_ares60262_en.pdf.

70. Kallings, "The First Postmodern Pandemic," 234.

71. TASO *Mission Statement*, 2011. Available online at: http://www.tasouganda.org/index.php?option=com_content&view=article&id=44:brief-background&catid=34.

72. John Maddox, "Does Duesberg Have A Right to Reply?" *Nature* 363 (1993): 109.

73. Samantha Power, "The Aids Rebel," *New Yorker*, May 19, 2003, 54–67.

74. A counter-orthodoxy that HIV does not cause AIDS is still to be found fairly prominently on the Internet and in parts of Africa, even among the educated elite. The current effectiveness of HAART treatment has done much to confirm the HIV theory and therefore counter the denialists, yet Duesberg himself has not conceded. See Pride Chigwedere and Max Essex, "AIDS Denialism and Public Health Practice," *AIDS and Behavior* 14 (2010): 23–47.

75. N. E. Groce and R. Trasi, "Rape of Individuals with Disability: AIDS and the Folk Belief of Virgin Cleansing," *The Lancet* 363 (2004): 1663–64.

76. G. J. Pitcher and D. M. G. Bowley, "Infant rape in South Africa," *The Lancet* 359 (2002): 274–75.

77. Groce and Trasi, "Rape of Individuals with Disability."

78. Rachel Jewkes, Jonathan Levin, Nolwazi Mbananga, and Debbie Bradshaw, "Rape of Girls in South Africa," *The Lancet* 359 (2002): 319–20; Rachel Jewkes, Lorna Martin, and Loveday Penn-Kekena, "The Virgin Cleansing Myth Cases of Child Rape are Not Exotic," *The Lancet* 359 (2002): 711.

79. Kallings, "The First Postmodern Pandemic," 223–24.

80. Nolen, *28 Stories*.

81. Power, "The AIDS Rebel," 56.

82. Sarah Joseph, "Trade and the Right to Health," in *Realizing the Right to Health*, ed. Clapham and Robinson.

83. Forbath, "Cultural Transformation."

84. Anthony Brink, "Criminal Complaint Of Genocide Against Abdurrazack 'Zackie' Achmat," 2007. Available online at: http://www.whale.to/b/brink3.html. For further discussion of the circumstance of this charge see Ben Goldacre, *Bad Science*, rev. ed. (London: Harper Perennial, 2009). Make sure that you read the revised

edition as the relevant chapter, "The Doctor Will Sue You Now," was omitted from the first printing because of a suit for libel from Matthias Rath, a vitamin pill entrepreneur, described by Goldacre as a colleague and employer of Brink. The chapter has also been made available by Goldacre and his publishers at: http://www.badscience.net/files/The-Doctor-Will-Sue-You-Now.pdf.

85. Republic of South Africa Constitution, 1996. Available online at: http://www.info.gov.za/documents/constitution/1996/96cons2.htm.

86. KwaZulu Natal, CCT32/97 (1997) ZACC 17: 1998 (1) SA 765 (CC). Available online at: http://www.saflii.org/za/cases/ZACC/1997/17.html.

87. Mark Heywood, "South Africa's Treatment Action Campaign: Combining Law and Social Mobilization to Realize the Right to Health," *Journal of Human Rights Practice* 1 (2009): 14–36.

88. Heywood, "South Africa's Treatment Action Campaign."

89. Forbath, "Cultural Transformation."

90. Heywood, "South Africa's Treatment Action Campaign," 17.

91. Ibid.; Forbath, "Cultural Transformations."

92. Kallings, "The First Postmodern Pandemic."

93. Dow and Essex, *Saturday*, ix.

94. Ibid., 61–66, 181–87.

95. Chigwedere and Essex, "Denialism," 243.

96. AVERT, "HIV and AIDS in Swaziland," 2011. Available online at: http://www.avert.org/aids-swaziland.htm#contentTable4.

97. Kallings, "The First Postmodern Pandemic," 226.

98. Nolen, *28 Stories*, 32.

99. There is at least one more promising, lower-tech, approach. Three randomized clinical trials, in Uganda, Kenya, and South Africa, show that male circumcision reduces the risk of female-to-male HIV transmission. B. Auvert et al., "Randomized, Controlled Intervention Trial of Male Circumcision for Reduction of HIV Infection Risk: The ANRS 1265 Trial," *PLoS Med* 2 (2005): e298; R. C. Bailey et al., "Male Circumcision for HIV Prevention in Young Men in Kisumu, Kenya: a Randomized Controlled Trial," *The Lancet* 369 (2007): 643–56; R. H. Gray et al., "Male Circumcision for HIV Prevention in Men in Rakai, Uganda: A Randomised Trial," *The Lancet* 369 (2007): 657–66.

There is, unfortunately, no evidence of direct reduction of male-to-female transmission, although it would seem to make sense that if fewer men are infected there will be less transmission to women.

However, if men think they are less at risk for HIV, they may then engage in riskier behavior. This is a general point about behavior in relation to risk. It has been argued that, for example, if you think you are driving a safe car you may well drive it at higher speed. John Adams, *Risk* (London: UCL Press, 1995).

It is an empirical claim, but brings home the point that those undergoing circumcision should be made aware that reducing risk is not the same as eliminating it. Furthermore, until the surgical wounds are healed, those circumcised are very much more vulnerable to infection than they otherwise would be, and so once again a belief that one is safe can be very dangerous.

100. Nolen, *28 Stories*, 113.
101. Lush, *Medical Totalitarianism*, 58.
102. Nolen, *28 Stories*.
103. Joseph S. Fulda, "The Mathematical Pull of Temptation," *Mind* 101 (1992): 305–07.

Chapter 4: Problems and Prospects

1. Joseph Stiglitz, *Globalization and Its Discontents* (New York: Norton, 2002).
2. Jennifer P. Ruger, "The Changing Role of the World Bank in Global Health," *American Journal of Public Health* 95 (2004): 60–70.
3. Stiglitz, *Globalization*, 11–20.
4. K. Abbasi, "The World Bank and World Health: Under Fire," *British Medical Journal* 318 (1999): 1003–06.
5. Lynn P. Freedman, "Drilling Down: Strengthening Local Health Systems to Address Global Health Crises," in *Realizing the Right to Health*, ed. Clapham and Robinson, 411.
6. Abbasi, "World Bank."
7. Hammonds and Ooms, "World Bank Policies," 36.
8. Ruger, "Changing Role," 68.
9. World Bank, *Investing in Health: The World Development Report for 1993* (Oxford: Oxford University Press, 1993), iii. Available online at: http://files.dcp2.org/pdf/WorldDevelopmentReport1993.pdf.
10. S. Anand and K. Hansen, "DALYs: Efficiency versus equity," *World Development* 26 (1998): 307–10. Opponents were especially critical of the application of the recently introduced and highly controversial DALY (disability-adjusted life-year) as a way of measuring health

and assessing cost-effectiveness. The DALY provides a measure of how much each health condition contributes to the "global burden of disease" and encourages health policy-makers to allocate funds to achieve the greatest reduction in the burden of disease for their health budget. This may seem entirely reasonable, but it has the consequence that attending to those with severe diseases that are very expensive to treat may yield less DALY reduction than alternative ways of spending the money, such as on common, less severe conditions that are relatively cheap to deal with.

11. World Bank, *Investing in Health*, iii.

12. Anne-Emanuelle Birn and Klaudia Dmitrienko, "The World Bank: Global Health Or Global Harm?" *American Journal of Public Health* 95 (2005): 1091.

13. Paul Collier, *The Bottom Billion* (Oxford: Oxford University Press, 2007).

14. Hammonds and Ooms, "World Bank Policies."

15. Ibid.

16. Fatma E. Marouf, "Holding The World Bank Accountable For Leakage Of Funds From Africa's Health Sector," *Health and Human Rights* 12 (2010): 95–107.

17. World Bank, *Improving Effectiveness and Outcomes for the Poor in Health, Nutrition, and Population* (2009), xi. Available online at: http://siteresources.worldbank.org/EXTWBASSHEANUTPOP/Resources/hnp_full_eval.pdf.

18. Ibid., 68.

19. Sarah Joseph, "Trade and the Right to Health."

20. Jane Galvao, "Brazil and Access to HIV/AIDS Drugs: A Question of Human Rights and Public Health," *American Journal of Public Health* 95 (2005): 1110–16.

21. Roy Porter, *The Greatest Benefit to Mankind* (London: HarperCollins, 1997), 23.

22. Ibid., 401.

23. Ibid., 427.

24. Ibid., 457–58.

25. World Health Organization, *Multidrug And Extensively Drug-Resistant TB (M/XDR-TB) 2010 Global Report On Surveillance And Response*, 2010, available online at: http://whqlibdoc.who.int/publications/2010/9789241599191_eng.pdf.

26. Farmer, *Pathologies of Power*, 123.

27. Ibid., 131.

28. Joseph, "Trade and the Right to Health."
29. Thomas Pogge, "The Health Impact Fund: How to Make New Medicines Accessible to All," in *Global Health Ethics*, ed. Solomon Benatar and Gillian Brock (Cambridge: Cambridge University Press, 2011).
30. WHO, *Multidrug Resistant TB*, 2.
31. Ibid., 3.
32. Olusoji Adeyi and Rifat Atun, "Universal Access to Malaria Medicines: Innovation in Financing and Delivery," *The Lancet* 376 (2010): 1869–71.
33. Nuffield Council on Bioethics, *The Ethics of Research Related to Healthcare in Developing Countries* (London: Nuffield Council on Bioethics, 2002), 31.
34. World Health Organization, *Working Together for Health* (2006). Available online at: http://www.who.int/whr/2006/whr06_en.pdf.
35. Amy Hagopian et al.,"The migration of physicians from sub-Saharan Africa to the United States of America: measures of the African brain drain," *Human Resources for Health* 2 (2004): 17.
36. Marvellous Mhloyi, "Health And Human Rights: An International Crusade," *Health and Human Rights* 1 (1994): 125–27.
37. King's Fund, *London Calling: The International Recruitment of Health Workers to the Capital* (London: King's Fund, 2004).
38. Hagopian, "Migration of Physicians."
39. Mary Robinson and Peggy Clark, "Forging Solutions to Health Worker Migration," *The Lancet* 371 (2008): 691–93.
40. World Health Organization, *Migration of Health Workers* (Fact Sheet No. 301), 2010. Available online at: http://www.who.int/mediacentre/factsheets/fs301/en/index.html.
41. Devesh Kapur and John McHale, *Give Us Your Best and Brightest: The Global Hunt for Talent and Its Impact on the Developing World* (Washington DC: Center for Global Development, 2005); and Gillian Brock, "Health in Developing Countries and Our Global Responsibilities," in *The Philosophy of Public Health*, ed. Angus Dawson (Farnham: Ashgate, 2009), 73–83.
42. Nigel Crisp, *Turning the World Upside Down* (London: Royal Society of Medicine Press, 2010), 73.
43. Ibid.
44. World Health Organization, *Global Code of Practice on the International Recruitment of Health Personnel*, 2010. Available online at: http://www.who.int/hrh/migration/code/code_en.pdf.

158   *Notes to pages 113–120*

45. World Health Organization, *Primary Health Care (Now More Than Ever)*, 2008. Available online at: http://www.who.int/whr/2008/en/index.html.
46. Anne Mills, "Mass Campaigns Versus General Health Services. What Have We Learnt in 40 Years about Vertical and Horizontal Approaches?" *Bulletin of the World Health Organization* 83 (2005): 315–16.
47. World Health Organization, *Primary Health Care*, 13.
48. World Health Organization, *Positive Synergies*, 2009. Available online at: http://www.who.int/healthsystems/GHIsynergies/en/index.html.
49. Global Forum on Health Research, *10/90 Gap*, 2011. Available online at: http://www.globalforumhealth.org/About/10-90-gap.
50. Nuffield Council on Bioethics, *Research in Developing Countries*, 15.
51. Paul Farmer and Nicole Gastineau Campos, "New Malaise: Bioethics and Human Rights in the Global Era," *Journal of Law, Medicine and Ethics* 32 (2004): 243.
52. Janice Hopkins Tanne, "President's commission considers how to protect human rights after Guatemala experiment," *British Medical Journal* 342 (2011): d3232. Full details are available at: http://www.hhs.gov/1946inoculationstudy/.
53. Marcia Angell, "The Ethics of Clinical Research in the Third World," *New England Journal of Medicine* 337 (1997): 847–49.
54. Robert L. Berger, "Nazi Science: The Dachau Hypothermia Experiments," *New England Journal of Medicine* 322 (1990): 1435–40.
55. World Medical Organization, "Declaration of Helsinki," *British Medical Journal* 313 (1996): 1448–49.
56. Nuffield Council on Bioethics, *Research in Developing Countries*.
57. Peter Lurie and Sidney M. Wolfe, "Unethical Trials of Interventions to Reduce Perinatal Transmission of the Human Immunodeficiency Virus in Developing Countries," *New England Journal of Medicine* 337 (1997): 855.
58. Angell, "Ethics of Clinical Research"; Farmer and Gastineau Campos, "New Malaise."
59. Nuffield Council on Bioethics, *Research in Developing Countries*, 92–95.
60. S. R. Benatar, "Imperialism, Research Ethics and Global Health," *Journal of Medical Ethics* 24 (1998): 221.
61. Nuffield Council on Bioethics, *Research in Developing Countries*, 115.
62. The current version, of 2008, qualifies this demand considerably,

stating in its place: "At the conclusion of the study, patients entered into the study are entitled to be informed about the outcome of the study and to share any benefits that result from it, for example, access to interventions identified as beneficial in the study or to other appropriate care or benefits." World Medical Association, *Declaration of Helsinki*, 2008 revision, available online at: http://www.wma.net/en/30publications/10policies/b3/index.html.

63. Ibid., 123.

64. Joseph Millum, "Post-Trial Access to Antiretrovirals: Who Owes What To Whom?" *Bioethics* 25 (2011): 145–54.

65. Leonard H. Glantz et al., "Research in Developing Countries: Taking 'Benefit' Seriously," *The Hastings Center Report* 28 (1998): 38–42.

66. Nuffield Council on Bioethics, *Research in Developing Countries*, 124.

67. Ibid., 203.

68. World Health Organization, UNICEF, UNFPA, and World Bank, *Joint Statement on Maternal Mortality and Newborn Health*, 2008. Available online at: http://www.unfpa.org/webdav/site/global/shared/safemotherhood/docs/jointstatement_mnh.pdf.

69. A. E. Yamin and D. P. Maine, "Maternal Mortality as a Human Rights Issue: Measuring Compliance with International Treaty Obligations," *Human Rights Quarterly* 21 (1999): 563–64.

70. United Nations, *Maternal Mortality Joint Statement*, 2009. Available online at: http://righttomaternalhealth.org/sites/iimmhr.civicactions.net/files/statement.pdf.

71. Amnesty International, *Demand Dignity*, 2010. Available online at: http://www.amnesty.org/en/campaigns/demand-dignity/issues/maternal-mortality/background.

72. Yamin and Maine, "Maternal Mortality"; United Nations, *Report of the Office of the United Nations High Commissioner for Human Rights on preventable maternal mortality and morbidity and human rights*, 2010. Available online at: http://www2.ohchr.org/english/bodies/hrcouncil/docs/14session/A.HRC.14.39.pdf.

73. World Health Organization Global Health Observatory, *Child Mortality*, 2011. Available online at: http://www.who.int/gho/mdg/child_mortality/situation_trends_child_mortality/en/index.html.

74. Yamin and Maine, "Maternal Mortality."

75. IIMMH, *Combating Maternal Mortality, Why Bring Human Rights into the Picture?*, 2009. Available online at: http://righttomaternalhealth.org/resource/HRC-panel-2009.

Chapter 5: Where Next?

1. Djély K. Samoura, "African Commission of Health and Human Rights Promoters," *Health and Human Rights* 2 (1995): 145–50; see also Cécile Marotte and Hervé Rakoto Razafimbahiny, "Haiti 1991–1994: The International Civilian Mission's Medical Unit," *Health and Human Rights* 2 (1995): 117–26.
2. David McCoy et al., "The Bill & Melinda Gates Foundation's Grant-making Programme for Global Health," *The Lancet* 373 (2009): 1645–53.
3. Elizabeth Pisani, "An End to Polio?" *Prospect*, March 2011, 72–74.
4. Richard Horton, "Stopping Malaria: The Wrong Road," review of Bill Shore, *The Imaginations of Unreasonable Men: Inspiration, Vision, and Purpose in the Quest to End Malaria*, *New York Review of Books*, February 24, 2011.
5. Farmer, *Pathologies of Power*, ix.
6. People's Health Movement, "About The People's Health Movement," 2011. Available online at: http://www.phmovement.org/en/about.

FURTHER READING

All books and papers mentioned appear in the bibliography.

INTRODUCTION

Paul Farmer, who features strongly in this book, is a health activist, anthropologist, and medical doctor. *Pathologies of Power* is a very impressive collection of his writings. His life story to date is told in Tracy Kidder's *Mountains Beyond Mountains*. Amartya Sen's own contribution to development is laid out in *Development as Freedom*. The World Bank's important *World Development Report* for 1993 is available from the World Bank website. For a detailed "state-of-the-art" survey concerning theory and practice in respect to the human right to health, see Andrew Clapham and Mary Robinson, eds., *Realizing the Human Right to Health*. A concise statement against the human right to health, entitled "Human Rights are the Wrong Basis for Health Care," is set out by William Easterly and is available from the *Financial Times* website on free registration.

CHAPTER 1

All covenants and declarations mentioned are easily available on the Internet. Mary Ann Glendon's *The World Made New* is very highly recommended. It is a beautifully written narrative of the drafting of the Universal Declaration of Human Rights and associated events. Johannes Morsink's *The Universal Declaration of Human Rights* is exceptionally impressive but much more for specialists. Norman Rockwell's *Four Freedoms* can be viewed widely on the Internet.

CHAPTER 2

I've looked in more detail at the different possible moral justifications for global action on health in a paper, "Global Justice and Health: The Basis of the Global Health Duty." Philosophers who have influenced the line taken in this book include Joseph Raz, in "Human Rights Without Foundations," Henry Shue, in *Basic Rights*, and Charles Beitz, in *The Idea of Human Rights*. For an important more critical philosophical approach to human rights, see Onora O'Neill, "The Dark Side of Human Rights."

CHAPTER 3

This chapter relies on the work of many scholars in health, human rights, and the history of medicine. Of those I have found most helpful, I would recommend in particular Peter Baldwin, *Disease and Democracy*, concerning the response to HIV/AIDS in the developed nations, and Paul Farmer, *AIDS and Accusation*, which focuses especially on Haiti. Unity Dow and Max Essex's book *Saturday is for Funerals* is a very unusual account of Botswana, alternating the narratives of Unity Dow, a judge and writer, with the more technically oriented writings of Max Essex, a leading HIV scientist. L. O. Kallings's "The First Postmodern Pandemic" is also very illuminating, as is Stephanie Nolen's *28 Stories of AIDS in Africa*. Jonathan Mann did perhaps more than anyone else to present HIV/AIDS in human rights terms; a good example of his writing is "Health and Human Rights."

CHAPTER 4

To keep up with current debates the free online journal *Health and Human Rights* is an excellent resource. Joseph Stiglitz's *Globalization and its Discontents* is a detailed critical discussion of the international financial institutions, and William Easterly's *The White Man's Burden* is an excellent broader critique of international government aid and development work. Dambisa Moyo's *Dead Aid* and Paul Collier's *The Bottom Billion* are essential reading on general development issues. On multi-drug-resistant TB and access to expensive medicines, see Paul Farmer, *Pathologies of Power*, and in particular his discussion of Russian prisons. On the international recruitment of skilled workers, see Kapur and McHale, *Give Us Your Brightest and Best*. The Nuffield Council on Bioethics report, *The Ethics of Research in Developing Countries* is an excellent guide to the vexed questions of international research ethics. A good introduction to issues regarding maternal mortality is A. E. Yamin and D. P. Maine, "Maternal Mortality as a Human Rights Issue: Measuring Compliance with International Treaty Obligations," and Amnesty International's "Demand Dignity" campaign, accessible through their website, has a wealth of information.

CHAPTER 5

The issue of global health governance has been a concern of the People's Health Movement. See, for example, Global Health Watch, *Alternative Health Report*, 2008. It was also discussed by the World Health Organization's Commission on the Social Determinants of Health, especially by the Globalization and Health Knowledge Network, in its report *Towards Health-Equitable Globalisation: Rights, Regulation and Redistribution.*

BIBLIOGRAPHY

Abbasi, K. "The World Bank and World Health: Under Fire." British Medical Journal 318 (1999): 1003–6.

Adams, John. *Risk*. London: UCL Press, 1995.

Adeyi, Olusoji, and Rifat Atun. "Universal Access to Malaria Medicines: Innovation in Financing and Delivery." *The Lancet* 376 (2010): 1869–71.

American Anthropological Association, Committee for Human Rights. "Declaration on Anthropology and Human Rights." 1999. http://www.aaanet.org/stmts/humanrts.htm (accessed July 21, 2010).

American Anthropological Association, The Executive Board. "Statement on Human Rights." *American Anthropologist* 49 (1947): 539–43.

Amnesty International. "Demand Dignity." 2010. http://www.amnesty.org/en/campaigns/demand-dignity/issues/maternal-mortality/background.

Amnesty International. *Uganda: Antihomosexuality Bill Is Inherently Discriminatory And Threatens Broader Human Rights*. London: Amnesty International, 2010.

Anand, S., and K. Hansen. "DALYs: Efficiency versus equity." *World Development* 26 (1998): 307–10.

Angell, Marcia. "The Ethics of Clinical Research in the Third World." *New England Journal of Medicine* 337(1997): 847–49.

Annas, George J. "Detention of HIV-Positive Haitians at Guantánamo." *New England Journal of Medicine* 329 (1993): 589–92.

——. "Human Rights and Health: the Universal Declaration of Human Rights at 50." *New England Journal of Medicine* 339 (1998): 1778–81.

Auvert, B., D. Taljaard, E. Lagarde, J. Sobngwi-Tambekou, R. Sitta, and A. Puren. "Randomized, Controlled Intervention Trial of Male Circumcision for Reduction of HIV Infection Risk: the ANRS 1265 Trial." *PLoS Med* 2 (2005): e298.

AVERT. "HIV and AIDS in Swaziland." 2011. http://www.avert.org/aids-swaziland.htm#contentTable4 (accessed August 4, 2011).

———. "HIV and AIDS Treatment in the UK." 2011. http://www.avert.org/hiv-treatment-uk.htm (accessed February 25, 2011).

———. "World AIDS Day" 2010. http://www.avert.org/world-aids-day.htm (accessed August 2, 2011).

Backman, Gunilla, Paul Hunt, Rajat Khosla, Camila Jaramillo-Strouss, Belachew Mekuria Fikre, Caroline Rumble, David Pevalin, David Acurio Páez, Mónica Armijos Pineda, Ariel Frisancho, Duniska Tarco, Mitra Motlagh, Dana Farcasanu, and Cristian Vladescu. "Health Systems and the Right to Health: An Assessment of 194 Countries." *The Lancet* 372 (2008): 2047–85.

Bailey, Robert C., Stephen Moses, Corette B. Parker, Kawango Agot, Ian Maclean, John N. Krieger, Carolyn F. M. Williams, Richard T. Campbell, and Jeckoniah O. Ndinya-Achola. "Male circumcision for HIV prevention in young men in Kisumu, Kenya: a randomized controlled trial." *The Lancet* 369 (2007): 643–56.

Baldwin, Peter. *Disease and Democracy*. Berkeley: University of California Press, 2005.

Bangkok Declaration. 1993. http://law.hku.hk/lawgovtsociety/Bangkok%20 Declaration.htm.(accessed August 3, 2011).

Battin, Margaret P., Leslie P. Francis, Jay A. Jacobson, and Charles B. Smith. *The Patient as Victim and Vector: Ethics and Infectious Disease*. Oxford: Oxford University Press, 2009.

Baumrin, Bernard. "Why There is No Right to Health Care." In *Medicine and Social Justice: Essays on the Distribution of Health Care,* edited by R. Rhodes, M. Pabst Battin, and A. Silvers. Oxford: Oxford University Press, 2002.

Beitz, Charles. *The Idea of Human Rights*. Oxford: Oxford University Press, 2009.

Benatar, S. R. "Human Rights in the Biotechnology Era 1." *BMC International Health and Human Rights* 2 (2002): 3.

———. "Imperialism, Research Ethics and Global Health." *Journal of Medical Ethics* 24 (1998): 221–22.

Benatar, S. R., A. Daar, and P. A. Singer. "Global Health: The Rationale for Mutual Caring." *International Affairs* 79 (2003): 107–38.

Benatar, Solomon, Stephen Gill, and Isabella Bakker. "Making Progress in Global Health: the Need for New Paradigms." *International Affairs* 85 (2009): 347–71.

Bentham, Jeremy. "Anarchical Fallacies" and "Supply Without Burden." 1796. In *Nonsense Upon Stilts,* edited by Jeremy Waldron. London: Methuen, 1987.

———. *An Introduction to the Principles of Morals and Legislation* (1781), edited by J. H. Burns and H. L. A. Hart. London: Athlone Press, 1970.

Berger, Robert L. "Nazi Science: The Dachau Hypothermia Experiments." *New England Journal of Medicine* 322 (1990): 1435–40.

Besson, Samantha, and John Tasioulas, eds. *The Philosophy of International Law.* Oxford: Oxford University Press, 2010.

Birn, Anne-Emanuelle. "Health and Human Rights: Historical Perspectives and Political Challenges." *Journal of Public Health Policy* 29 (2008): 32–41.

Birn, Anne-Emanuelle, and Klaudia Dmitrienko. "The World Bank: Global Health or Global Harm?" *American Journal of Public Health* 95 (2005): 1091.

Brink, Anthony. "Criminal Complaint Of Genocide Against Abdurrazack 'Zackie' Achmat." 2007. http://www.whale.to/b/brink3.html (accessed February 20, 2011).

Brock, Gillian. *Global Justice.* Oxford: Oxford University Press, 2009.

———. "Health in Developing Countries and Our Global Responsibilities." In *The Philosophy of Public Health,* edited by Angus Dawson. Farnham: Ashgate, 2009, 73–83.

Burnham, Gilbert, Riyadh Lafta, Shannon Doocy, and Les Roberts. "Mortality after the 2003 Invasion of Iraq: A Cross-sectional Cluster Sample Survey." *The Lancet* 368 (2006): 1421–28.

Caney, Simon. *Justice Beyond Borders.* Oxford: Oxford University Press, 2005.

Central Intelligence Agency. "The World Factbook: Life Expectancy at Birth." 2009. https://www.cia.gov/library/publications/the-world-factbook/rankorder/2102rank.html (accessed November 25, 2009).

Chigwedere, Pride, and Max Essex. "AIDS Denialism and Public Health Practice." *AIDS and Behavior* 14 (2010): 237–47.

Childress, James F., Ruth R. Faden, Ruth D. Gaare, Lawrence O. Gostin, Jeffrey Kahn, Richard J. Bonnie, Nancy E. Kass, Anna C. Mastroianni, Jonathan D. Moreno, and Phillip Nieburg, "Public Health Ethics: Mapping the Terrain." *The Journal of Law, Medicine & Ethics* 30 (2002): 170–78.

Clapham, Andrew, and Mary Robinson, eds. *Realizing the Right to Health.* Zurich: Rüffer & Rub, 2009.

Collier, Paul. *The Bottom Billion.* Oxford: Oxford University Press, 2007.

Collins, Daryl, Jonathan Morduch, Stuart Rutherford, and Orlanda Ruthven. *Portfolios of the Poor: How the World's Poor Live on $2 a Day.* Princeton: Princeton University Press, 2009.

Conference on Primary Health Care. *Declaration of Alma-Ata.* 1978. http://www.who.int/hpr/NPH/docs/declaration_almaata.pdf (accessed March 19, 2011).

Cooper, John F. "Peking's Post-Tiananmen Foreign Policy: The Human Rights Factor." *Issues and Studies* 30 (1994): 69.

Crewe, Mary. "The HIV/AIDS Epidemic and Human Rights Responses." In Clapham and Robinson, *Realizing the Right to Health.*

Crisp, Nigel. *Turning the World Upside Down.* London: Royal Society of Medicine Press, 2010.

Daniels, Norman. "Equity and Population Health: Toward a Broader Bioethics Agenda." *The Hastings Center Report* 36 (2006): 22–23.

Donnelly, Jack. "Human Rights and Asian Values: A Defence of 'Western' Universalism." In *The East Asian Challenge For Human Rights,* edited by Joanne R. Bauer and Daniel A. Bell. Cambridge: Cambridge University Press, 1999.

Dournon, E., et al. "Effects Of Zidovudine In 365 Consecutive Patients With Aids Or Aids-Related Complex." *The Lancet* 332 (1988): 1297–302.

Dow, Unity, and Max Essex. *Saturday Is for Funerals.* Cambridge, MA: Harvard University Press, 2010.

Easterly, William. "Human Rights Are the Wrong Basis for Health Care." *Financial Times,* October 12, 2009. http://www.ft.com/cms/s/0/89bbbda2-b763-11de-9812-00144feab49a.html (accessed November 25, 2009).

———. *The White Man's Burden.* Oxford: Oxford University Press, 2006.

Eggers, P. W. "Medicare's End Stage Renal Disease Program." *Health Care Financing Review* 22 (2000): 55–60.

Farmer, Paul. *Aids and Accusation.* Berkeley: University of California Press, 1992.

———. *Pathologies of Power.* Berkeley: University of California Press, 2005.

Farmer, Paul, and Nicole Gastineau Campos. "New Malaise: Bioethics and Human Rights in the Global Era." *Journal of Law, Medicine and Ethics* 32 (2004): 243–51.

Ferraz, Octavio. "The Right To Health In The Courts Of Brazil: Worsening Health Inequities?" *Health and Human Rights* 11 (2009): 33–45.

Fischl, Margaret A., Douglas D. Richman, Michael H. Grieco, Michael S. Gottlieb, Paul A. Volberding, Oscar L. Laskin, John M. Leedom, Jerome E. Groopman, Donna Mildvan, Robert T. Schooley, George G. Jackson, David T. Durack, Dannie King, and The AZT Collaborative Working Group, "The Efficacy of Azidothymidine (AZT) in the Treatment of Patients with AIDS and AIDS-Related Complex." *New England Journal of Medicine* 317 (1987): 185–91.

Forbath, William E. "Cultural Transformation, Deep Institutional Reform, and ESR Practice." In *Stones of Hope: African Lawyers Use Human Rights to Challenge Global Poverty*, edited by Jeremy Perelman and Lucie White. Stanford, CA: Stanford University Press, 2011.

Foreman, Lisa. " 'Rights' and Wrongs: What Utility for the Right to Health in Reforming Trade Rules on Medicines?" *Health and Human Rights* 10 (2008): 37–53.

Freedman, Lynn P. "Drilling Down: Strengthening Local Health Systems to Address Global Health Crises." In Clapham and Robinson, *Realizing the Right to Health*.

Freeman, Michael. *Human Rights*. Cambridge: Polity, 2002.

Frøland, S. S., P. Jenum, C. F. Lindboe, K. W. Wefring, P. J. Linnestad, and T. Böhmer. "HIV-1 Infection in Norwegian Family before 1970." *The Lancet* 331 (June 11, 1988): 1344–45.

Fulda, Joseph S. "The Mathematical Pull of Temptation." *Mind* 101 (1992): 305–7.

Gallo, Robert C. "A Reflection on HIV/AIDS research after 25 Years." *Retrovirology* 3 (2006): 72.

Galvao, Jane. "Brazil and Access to HIV/AIDS Drugs: A Question of Human Rights and Public Health." *American Journal of Public Health* 95, no. 7 (2005): 1110–16.

Garrett, Laurie. *The Coming Plague*. London: Virago, 1995.

Gauri, Varun, and Dan Brinks, eds. *Courting Social Justice*. Cambridge: Cambridge University Press, 2008.

Gilbert, M., P. Thomas, Andrew Rambaut, Gabriela Wlasiuk, Thomas J. Spira, Arthur E. Pitchenik, and Michael Worobey. "The Emergence of HIV/AIDS in the Americas and Beyond." *Proceedings of the National Academy of Science* 104 (2007): 18566–70.

Glantz, Leonard H., George T. Annas, Michael A. Grodin, and Wendy K. Mariner. "Research in Developing Countries: Taking 'Benefit' Seriously." *Hastings Center Report* 28 (1998): 38–42.

Glendon, Mary Ann. *A World Made New: Eleanor Roosevelt and the Universal Declaration of Human Rights*. New York: Random House, 2001.

Global Forum on Health Research. *10/90 Gap.* 2011. http://www.global-forumhealth.org/About/10-90-gap (accessed March 13, 2010).

Global Health Watch. *Alternative World Health Report 2.* London: Zed Books, 2008.

Goldacre, Ben. *Bad Science.* Revised ed. London: Harper Perennial, 2009.

Gray, Ronald H., Godfrey Kigozi, David Serwadda, Frederick Makumbi, Stephen Watya, Fred Nalugoda, Noah Kiwanuka, Lawrence H. Moulton, Mohammad A. Chaudhary, Michael Z. Chen, Nelson K. Sewankambo, Fred Wabwire-Mangen, Melanie C. Bacon, Carolyn F. M. Williams, Pius Opendi, Steven J. Reynolds, Oliver Laeyendecker, Thomas C. Quinn and Maria J. Wawer, "Male Circumcision for HIV Prevention in Men in Rakai, Uganda: A Randomised Trial." *The Lancet* 369 (2007): 657–66.

Griffin, James. "Discrepancies Between the Best Philosophical Account of Human Rights and the International Law of Human Rights." *Proceedings of the Aristotelian Society* 101 (2001): 1–28.

———. *On Human Rights.* Oxford: Oxford University Press, 2008.

Groce, N. E., and R. Trasi. "Rape of Individuals with Disability: AIDS and the Folk Belief of Virgin Cleansing." *The Lancet* 363 (2004): 1663–64.

Haacker, Markus. "The Macroeconomics of HIV/AIDS." In *Southern Africa: 2020 Vision,* edited by M. Hannam and J. Wolff. London: e9 Publishing, 2010.

Hagopian, Amy, Matthew J. Thompson, Meredith Fordyce, Karin E. Johnson and L. Gary Hart. "The Migration of Physicians from Sub-Saharan Africa to the United States of America: Measures of the African Brain Drain." *Human Resources for Health* 2 (2004): 17.

Hammonds, Rachel, and Gorik Ooms. "World Bank Policies and the Obligation of its Members to Respect, Protect and Fulfill the Right to Health." *Human Rights and Health* 8 (2004): 26–60.

Hessler, Kristin, and Allen Buchanan. "Specifying the Content of the Human Right to Health Care." In *Medicine and Social Justice: Essays on the Distribution of Health Care,* edited by R. Rhodes, M. Pabst Battin, and A. Silvers. Oxford: Oxford University Press, 2002.

Heywood, Mark. "South Africa's Treatment Action Campaign: Combining Law and Social Mobilization to Realize the Right to Health." *Journal of Human Rights Practice* 1 (2009): 14–36.

Hopkins Tanne, Janice. "President's Commission Considers How to Protect Human Rights after Guatemala Experiment." *British Medical Journal* 342 (2011): d3232.

Horton, Richard. "Stopping Malaria: The Wrong Road." Review of Bill

Shore, *The Imaginations of Unreasonable Men: Inspiration, Vision, and Purpose in the Quest to End Malaria. New York Review of Books*, February 24, 2011.

Huminer, D., J. B. Rosenfeld, and S. D. Pitlik. "AIDS in the pre-AIDS era." *Review of Infectious Diseases* 9 (1987): 1102–8.

International Initiative on Maternal Mortality and Human Rights, *Combating Maternal Mortality, Why Bring Human Rights into the Picture?* 2009. http://righttomaternalhealth.org/resource/HRC-panel-2009 (accessed March 5, 2011).

James, C. L. R. *The Black Jacobins.* 1938. London: Penguin, 2001.

Jewkes, Rachel, Jonathan Levin, Nolwazi Mbananga, and Debbie Bradshaw. "Rape of Girls in South Africa." *The Lancet* 359 (2002): 319–20.

Jewkes, Rachel, Martin Lorna, and Loveday Penn-Kekena. "The Virgin Cleansing Myth Cases of Child Rape are Not Exotic." *The Lancet* 359 (2002): 711.

Joffe, Helene. *Risk and the Other.* Cambridge: Cambridge University Press, 1999.

Joseph, Sarah. "Trade and the Right to Health." In Clapham and Robinson, *Realizing the Right to Health.*

Kallings, L. O. "The First Postmodern Pandemic: 25 years of HIV/AIDS." Review. *Journal of International Medicine* 263 (2008): 218–43.

Kapur, Devesh, and John McHale. *Give Us Your Best and Brightest: The Global Hunt for Talent and Its Impact on the Developing World.* Washington, DC: Center for Global Development, 2005.

Kidder, Tracy. *Mountains Beyond Mountains.* New York: Random House, 2003.

King's Fund. *London Calling: The International Recruitment of Health Workers to the Capital.* London: King's Fund, 2004.

Kirby, Michael. "The New AIDS Virus—Ineffective and Unjust Laws." *Journal of Acquired Immune Deficiency Syndromes* 1 (1988): 304–12.

KwaZulu Natal, CCT32/97 (1997) ZACC 17: 1998 (1) SA 765 (CC), available online at: http://www.saflii.org/za/cases/ZACC/1997/17.html.

Locke, John. *Two Treatises of Government.* 1689. Cambridge: Cambridge University Press, 1988.

Lurie, Peter, and Sidney M. Wolfe. "Unethical Trials of Interventions to Reduce Preinatal Transmission of the Human Immunodeficiency Virus in Developing Countries." *New England Journal of Medicine* 337 (1997): 853–55.

Lush, David. "Medical Totalitarianism and My Part in Its Downfall." In *Southern Africa: 2020 Vision*, edited by M. Hannam and J. Wolff. London: e9 Publishing, 2010.

MacIntyre, Alasdair. *After Virtue.* London: Duckworth, 1981.

Maddox, John. "Does Duesberg Have A Right to Reply?" *Nature* 363 (1993): 109.

Malik, Charles. "Talk on Human Rights." 1949. http://www.udhr.org/history/talkon.htm (accessed August 4, 2011).

Mallaby, Sebastian. *The World's Banker.* New Haven: Yale University Press, 2004.

Mann, Jonathan M. "Human Rights and AIDS: The Future of the Pandemic." In *Health and Human Rights,* by Jonathan M. Mann, Sofia Gruskin, Michael A. Grodin, and George J. Annas. London: Routledge, 1999.

Mann, Jonathan M., Lawrence Gostin, Sofia Gruskin, Troyen Brennan, Zita Lazzarini, and Harvey Fineberg. "Health and Human Rights." In *Health and Human Rights,* by Jonathan M. Mann, Sofia Gruskin, Michael A. Grodin, and George J. Annas. London: Routledge, 1999.

Maritain, Jacques. *Man and the State.* Chicago: University of Chicago Press, 1951.

Marotte, Cécile, and Hervé Rakoto Razafimbahiny. "Haiti 1991–1994: The International Civilian Mission's Medical Unit." *Health and Human Rights* 2 (1995): 117–26.

Marouf, Fatma E. "Holding the World Bank Accountable for Leakage of Funds from Africa's Health Sector." *Health and Human Rights* 12 (2010): 95–107.

Marx, Karl. "On the Jewish Question." 1843. In *Early Writings,* edited by L. Colletti. Harmondsworth: Penguin, 1975.

McCoy, David, Gayatri Kembhavi, Jinesh Patel, and Akish Luintel. "The Bill & Melinda Gates Foundation's Grant-making Programme for Global Health." *The Lancet* 373 (2009): 1645–53.

Mhloyi, Marvellous. "Health And Human Rights: An International Crusade." *Health and Human Rights* 1 (1994): 125–27.

Mills, Anne. "Mass Campaigns Versus General Health Services. What Have We Learnt in 40 Years about Vertical and Horizontal Approaches?" *Bulletin of the World Health Organization* 83 (2005): 315–16.

Millum, Joseph. "Post-Trial Access to Antiretrovirals: Who Owes What To Whom?" *Bioethics* 25 (2011): 145–54.

Morsink, Johannes. *The Universal Declaration of Human Rights: Origins, Drafting and Intent.* Philadelphia: University of Pennsylvania Press, 1999.

Moyo, Dambisa. *Dead Aid.* London: Allen Lane, 2009.

National Association of People Living with AIDS and HIV. "The Den-

ver Principles 1983 and Today." 2011. http://www.napwa.org/content/
denver-principles-1983-and-today (accessed February 25, 2011).

National Planning Commission of Namibia. *Namibia Vision 2030.* 2004.
http://www.npc.gov.na/vision/vision_2030bgd.htm (accessed March
19, 2011).

Nickel, James. "Human Rights." In *The Stanford Encyclopedia of Philosophy*,
edited by Edward N. Zalta. 2009. http://plato.stanford.edu/archives/
spr2009/entries/rights-human (accessed August 4, 2011).

Nolen, Stephanie. *28 Stories of AIDS in Africa.* London: Portobello Books,
2007.

Nozick, Robert. *Anarchy, State, and Utopia.* Oxford: Blackwell, 1974.

Nuffield Council on Bioethics. *The Ethics of Research Related to Healthcare
in Developing Countries.* London: Nuffield Council on Bioethics, 2002.

O'Neill, Onora. "The Dark Side of Human Rights." *International Affairs*
81 (2005): 427–39.

———. "Public Health or Clinical Ethics: Thinking Beyond Borders." *Ethics and International Affairs* 16 (2002): 35–45.

Orbinski, James. *An Imperfect Offering.* London: Rider, 2008.

People's Health Movement. "About The People's Health Movement."
2011. http://www.phmovement.org/en/about (accessed March 19,
2011).

Piot, Peter, Susan Timberlake, and Jason Sigurdson. "Governance and
the Response to AIDS: Lessons for Development and Human Rights."
In Clapham and Robinson, *Realizing the Right to Health.*

Pisani, Elizabeth. "An End to Polio?" *Prospect*, March 2011, 72–74.

Pitcher, G. J., and D. M. G. Bowley. "Infant Rape in South Africa." *The
Lancet* 359 (2002): 274–75.

Pogge, Thomas. "The Health Impact Fund: How to Make New Medicines Accessible to All." In *Global Health Ethics*, edited by Solomon
Benatar and Gillian Brock. Cambridge: Cambridge University Press,
2011.

———. "Human Rights and Global Health: A Research Programme."
Metaphilosophy 36 (2005): 182–209.

———. *World Poverty and Human Rights.* Cambridge, MA: Cambridge University Press, 2002.

Porter, Roy. *The Greatest Benefit to Mankind.* London: HarperCollins, 1997.

Power, Samantha. "The Aids Rebel," *The New Yorker*, May 19, 2003, 54–67.

Rawls, John. *The Law of Peoples.* Cambridge, MA: Harvard University
Press, 1999.

———. *Political Liberalism*. 1993. New York: Columbia University Press, 1996.

———. *A Theory of Justice*. Cambridge, MA: Harvard University Press, 1971.

Raz, Joseph. "Human Rights Without Foundations." In *The Philosophy of International Law*, edited by J. Tasioulas and S. Besson. Oxford: Oxford University Press, 2010.

Republic of South Africa Constitution. 1996. http://www.info.gov.za/doc uments/constitution/1996/96cons2.htm (accessed November 26, 2009).

Richman, Douglas D., Margaret A. Fischl, Michael H. Grieco, Michael S. Gottlieb, Paul A. Volberding, Oscar L. Laskin, John M. Leedom, Jerome E. Groopman, Donna Mildvan, Martin S. Hirsch, George G. Jackson, David T. Durack, Sandra Nusinoff-Lehrman, and the AZT Collaborative Working Group. "The Toxicity of Azidothymidine (AZT) in the Treatment of Patients with AIDS and AIDS-Related Complex." *New England Journal of Medicine* 317 (1987): 192–97.

Robinson, Mary, and Peggy Clark. "Forging Solutions to Health Worker Migration." *The Lancet* 371 (2008): 691–93.

Ruger, Jennifer P. "The Changing Role of the World Bank in Global Health." *American Journal of Public Health* 95 (2004): 60–70.

Samoura, Djély K. "African Commission Of Health And Human Rights Promoters." *Health and Human Rights* 2 (1995): 145–50.

Sen, Amartya. *Development as Freedom*. Oxford: Oxford University Press, 1999.

———. *Human Rights and Asian Values*. New York: Carnegie Council on Ethics and International Affairs, 1997.

———. Foreword to Paul Farmer, *Pathologies of Power*. 2005.

Shue, Henry. *Basic Rights*. 2nd edition. Princeton: Princeton University Press, 1996.

Singer, Peter. "Famine, Affluence and Morality." *Philosophy and Public Affairs* 1 (1972): 229–43.

SouthAfrica.Info. "MySonDiedofAIDS:Mandela."January12,2005.http:// www.southafrica.info/mandela/mandela-son.htm (accessed August 3, 2011).

Sreenivasan, Gopal. "International Justice and Health: A Proposal." *Ethics and International Affairs* 16 (2002): 81–90.

Steiner, H. "Territorial Justice and Global Redistribution." In *The Political Philosophy of Cosmopolitanism*, edited by G. Brock and H. Brighouse, 28–38. Cambridge: Cambridge University Press, 2005.

Stiglitz, Joseph. *Globalization and Its Discontents*. New York: Norton, 2002.

The AIDS Support Organisation (TASO). "Mission Statement."

2011.http://www.tasouganda.org/index.php?option=com_content&view
=article&id=44:brief-background&catid=34 (accessed February 19,
2011).

UNAIDS. *The Greater Involvement of People Living With HIV* (GIPA). 2007.
http://data.unaids.org/pub/BriefingNote/2007/jc1299_policy_brief_
gipa.pdf (accessed February 25, 2011).

United Nations. *Convention on the Rights of the Child.* 1989. http://www2.
ohchr.org/english/law/crc.htm (accessed November 26, 2009).

——. *General Comment 3.* 1990. http://www.unhchr.ch/tbs/doc.nsf/(symbol)/
E.C.12.2000.4.En (accessed November 26, 2009).

——. *General Comment 14.* 2000. http://www.unhchr.ch/tbs/doc.nsf/(symbol)
/E.C.12.2000.4.En (accessed November 26, 2009).

——. *General Comment 17.* 2005. http://www.unhchr.ch/tbs/doc.nsf/(Symbol)/
E.C.12.GC.17.En?OpenDocument. (accessed August 4, 2011).

——. *International Covenant on Economic, Social, and Cultural Rights.* 1966.
http://www2.ohchr.org/english/law/cescr.htm (accessed November 26,
2009).

——. *Maternal Mortality Joint Statement.* 2009. http://righttomaternalhealth.
org/sites/iimmhr.civicactions.net/files/statement.pdf (accessed March
4, 2011).

——. *Political Declaration on HIV/AIDS.* 2006. http://data.unaids.org/pub/
Report/2006/20060615_hlm_politicaldeclaration_ares60262_en.pdf
(accessed February 25, 2011).

——. *Report of the Office of the United Nations High Commissioner for Human Rights
on Preventable Maternal Mortality and Morbidity and Human Rights.* 2010.
http://www2.ohchr.org/english/bodies/hrcouncil/docs/14session/A.
HRC.14.39.pdf (accessed March 6, 2011).

——. *United Nations Treaty Collection.* 2011. http://treaties.un.org/Pages/View-
Details.aspx?src=TREATY&mtdsg_no=IV-3-a&chapter=4&lang=en
(accessed March 19, 2011).

——. *Universal Declaration of Human Rights.* 1948. http://www.un.org/en/
documents/udhr/ (accessed November 26, 2009).

UNICEF. *Convention on the Rights of the Child: Frequently Asked Questions.*
2006. http://www.unicef.org/crc/index_30229.html (accessed November 26, 2009).

United States Government. *Response to Request.* No date. http://www.glo-
balgovernancewatch.org/docLib/20080213_US_Hunt_Response.pdf
(accessed November 26, 2009).

Weeks, B. S., and I. E. Alcamo. *AIDS: The Biological Basis.* 5th edition.
Sudbury, MA: Jones and Bartlett, 2010.

White, Ryan, and Ann Marie Cunningham. *My Own Story.* New York: Penguin, 1991.

Wise, Paul. "Child Beauty, Child Rights and the Devaluation of Women." *Health and Human Rights* 1 (1994): 472–76.

Wolff, Jonathan. "Global Justice and Health: The Basis of the Global Health Duty." In *Global Justice and Bioethics,* edited by E. Emanuel and J. Mullian. Oxford: Oxford University Press, forthcoming.

Wolff, Jonathan, and Avner de-Shalit. *Disadvantage.* Oxford: Oxford University Press, 2007.

Woodman, Zenda, and Carolyn Williamson. "HIV Molecular Epidemiology: Transmission and Adaptation to Human Populations." *Current Opinion in HIV and AIDS* 4 (2009): 247–52.

World Bank. *Improving Effectiveness and Outcomes for the Poor in Health, Nutrition, and Population.* 2009. http://siteresources.worldbank.org/EXTW BASSHEANUTPOP/Resources/hnp_full_eval.pdf (accessed March 6, 2011).

———. *Investing in Health: The World Development Report for 1993.* Oxford: Oxford University Press, 1993. http://files.dcp2.org/pdf/WorldDevelopmentReport1993.pdf (accessed August 4, 2011).

World Health Organization. *Chronicle of the World Health Organization.* 1947. http://whqlibdoc.who.int/hist/chronicles/chronicle_1947.pdf (accessed August 4, 2011).

———. *Constitution.* 1946. http://www.who.int/governance/eb/who_constitution_en.pdf (accessed November 26, 2009).

———. *The WHO Global Code of Practice on the International Recruitment of Health Personnel.* 2010. http://www.who.int/hrh/migration/code/code_en.pdf (accessed August 4, 2011).

———. *Migration of Health Workers* (Fact Sheet No. 301). 2010. http://www.who.int/mediacentre/factsheets/fs301/en/index.html (accessed August 4, 2011).

———. *Multidrug and Extensively Drug-Resistant TB (M/XDR-TB) 2010 Global Report on Surveillance and Response.* 2010. http://whqlibdoc.who.int/publications/2010/9789241599191_eng.pdf (accessed August 4, 2011).

———. *Positive Synergies.* 2009. http://www.who.int/healthsystems/GHIsynergies/en/index.html (accessed December 6, 2009).

———. *Primary Health Care (Now More Than Ever).* 2008. http://www.who.int/whr/2008/en/index.html (accessed March 11, 2011).

———. *World Health Report: Health Systems: Improving Performance.* Geneva: World Health Organization, 2000. http://www.who.int/whr/2000/en/whr00_annex_en.pdf (accessed March 19, 2011).

———. *Working Together for Health*. 2006. http://www.who.int/whr/2006/whr06_en.pdf (accessed June 23, 2011).

World Health Organization, Commission on the Social Determinants of Health, Globalization Knowledge Network. *Towards Health-Equitable Globalisation: Rights, Regulation and Redistribution*. 2007. http://www.who.int/social_determinants/resources/gkn_final_report_042008.pdf (accessed June 24, 2011).

World Health Organization, UNICEF, UNFPA, and World Bank. *Joint Statement on Maternal Mortality and Newborn Health*. 2008. http://www.unfpa.org/webdav/site/global/shared/safemotherhood/docs/jointstatement_mnh.pdf (accessed March 4, 2011).

World Medical Association. *Declaration of Helsinki*. 2000 revision. *Journal of the American Medical Association* 284 (2000): 3043-45.

World Medical Association. *Declaration of Helsinki*. 2008 revision. http://www.wma.net/en/30publications/10policies/b3/ (accessed August 4, 2011).

Yamin, A. E., and D. P. Maine. "Maternal Mortality as a Human Rights Issue: Measuring Compliance with International Treaty Obligations." *Human Rights Quarterly* 21 (1999): 563–607.

ACKNOWLEDGMENTS

First, a confession. As a political philosopher, I have long been skeptical about the idea of human rights. Rights language had been appropriated by the libertarian right, and in much of my work I preferred to focus on concepts such as social justice or disadvantage. But increasingly I worried that my academic work was out of step with the global political agitators I most admired, such as Amnesty International and Human Rights Watch. Intellectually, the most important step for me was listening to Joseph Raz argue that philosophical work on human rights should be reoriented around human rights practice and give up its obsession with the question of the philosophical foundations of human rights. Reading and listening to Gorik Ooms and Paul Hunt reinforced me in this attitude, which I also recognize in the philosophical writings especially of Henry Shue and Charles Beitz, among many others. I've been slow to come to the human rights party, but I'm very pleased that I am here at last.

The idea of writing this book came from discussions, over several years, with Roby Harrington at Norton. We had long agreed that I should write something for Norton, and the Global Ethics series presented the ideal opportunity. I am immensely grateful to Roby for his encouragement and confidence, and to Anthony Appiah for his support. Writing this book allowed me to do what I find I like immensely: learn from people in academic disciplines other than my own, including health activists, international lawyers, clinicians, anthropologists and medical historians.

A draft of this book was read by Doug Reeve, Mark Hannam, Markus Haacker, and Octavio Luiz Motta Ferraz, who saved me from many mistakes and provided excellent positive suggestions. Advice on revisions from Roby Harrington, Anthony Appiah, Brendan Curry, and Jake Schindel was invaluable. Some of my earlier work on this topic was greatly assisted by comments from Gillian Brock and Solly Benatar. I'd also like to thank Allegra Huston for her superb copyediting. Chance conversations that alerted me to important issues that I might otherwise have missed took place with Ole Frithjof Norheim, in a hotel bar, and Polly Vizard, on, I think, a train. I've also learned more than I can remember, and certainly more than I can remember to acknowledge, in seminar rooms and lecture halls, both from other speakers and from audiences at my own talks.

INDEX

Page numbers beginning with 141 refer to notes.